JOSEPH STALIN

and the

Soviet Union

JOSEPH STALIN
and the
Soviet Union

Kevin Cunningham

MORGAN
REYNOLDS
PUBLISHING
Greensboro, North Carolina

WORLD LEADERS

GEORGE C. MARSHALL
ADOLF HITLER
WOODROW WILSON
VACLAV HAVEL
GENGHIS KHAN
JOSEPH STALIN
CHE GUEVARA

JOSEPH STALIN AND THE SOVIET UNION

Copyright © 2006 by Kevin Cunningham

Library of Congress Cataloging-in-Publication Data

Cunningham, Kevin, 1966-
   Joseph Stalin and the Soviet Union / Kevin Cunningham.
       p. cm.
   Includes bibliographical references and index.
   ISBN-13: 978-1-931798-94-5 (library binding)
   ISBN-10: 1-931798-94-X (library binding)
   1. Stalin, Joseph, 1879-1953. 2. Heads of state—Soviet Union—
Biography. 3. Soviet Union—Politics and government,—1917-1936. 4.
Soviet Union—Politics and government—1936-1953. I. Title.
   DK268.S8C86 2006
   947.084'2092—dc22

                        2005032540

Printed in the United States of America
First Edition

To Elizabeth

CONTENTS

Joseph Stalin. (Library of Congress)

One
STUDENT
REVOLUTIONARY

In January 1913, a man with three names arrived in Vienna. His oldest acquaintances knew him by his birth name, Joseph Djugashvili, as did the Russian secret police, the Okhrana. Those in the Marxist underground working to overthrow Russia's Tsarist government usually called him Koba, an alias he had taken from his favorite novel. Recently, though, he had been using a new, stronger name—Stalin, the Man of Steel.

Stalin was visiting Vienna, the imperial city of the aged Austrian-Hungarian Empire, on the orders of Vladimir Ilyich Ulyanov (who used the alias Lenin), the leader of the Bolsheviks, the most radical of the Russian Marxist groups. Lenin had asked Stalin to go to Vienna to research and write a paper on the issues presented by

Vienna was one of the cultural and political hubs of Europe in the early twentieth century. (Library of Congress)

the large number of non-Russian national groups that lived within the Russian Empire. This was an opportunity for Stalin to advance by proving his intellectual skills. Before this he had been a "practical," one who focused on the nuts and bolts of the organization.

For a month, Stalin gathered data from Vienna's libraries. He needed help with some of the foreign languages, particularly German, and comrades in the city assisted him with translations. This gave him the opportunity to socialize with others in the movement. He saw firsthand the life of the café revolutionaries who had worked in libraries and argued in coffeehouses while he lived among laborers and in Siberian exile. If Stalin resented their easier life, he kept it to himself. Later, when he became supreme ruler of the Soviet Union, few who knew him then could recall anything of his days in Vienna.

Three significant figures in Stalin's life were in Vienna in 1913, a year before the outbreak of World War I, which would destroy both the Austrian and Russian empires. Two of the figures were Russian. Nikolai Bukharin was a Bolshevik ally who would later be executed on Stalin's orders. Leon Trotsky was a professional Marxist revolutionary and one of Lenin's fieriest opponents in the movement. Stalin's secret police would murder him in 1940.

The other figure was an Austrian, who was soon to move to Munich. Adolf Hitler had lived the miserable life of a failed artist for years in Vienna, but World War I would set him on the path toward total political power in his adopted country of Germany.

When it was completed, Stalin's essay "Marxism and the National Question" impressed Lenin. Stalin had passed the test and now had an intellectual niche in Lenin's hierarchy.

When Stalin was born in 1878, the Russian Empire stretched from Finland in the far north to Armenia in the south, from Poland in the west to the Kamchatka Peninsula on the Pacific Ocean. Yet despite its size, Russia was stuck in the past, particularly when compared to the rapidly developing nations of Western Europe. Serfdom, a form of slavery that was a relic of medieval society in most of Europe, had officially existed in Russia until the 1860s and lingered on in some regions until the twentieth century. The West, by contrast, was undergoing the Industrial Revolution. Assembly-line workers in factories were replacing artisans and tradesman, and vast numbers of the population were leaving the countryside to work in giant cities.

In 1878, Russia still had few factories and remained overwhelmingly rural. The vast majority of the empire's 125 million citizens were poor and illiterate peasants working the land with primitive tools.

The political differences were equally profound. Whereas the West had turned toward representative government, the Romanov family ruled Russia as they had for centuries—as absolute monarchs guided by laws laid down in 1716 by the most legendary of the czars, Peter the Great.

One of the lands relying on the czar's goodwill was Georgia, a pleasant country east of the Black Sea that bordered the Caucasus Mountains. Much of the sunny, pleasantly warm land sat in a fertile river valley good for growing grains, such as wheat and oats, and fruit, including peaches, apricots, and grapes.

To the ancient Greeks, Georgia was home to the gods. Zeus, the king of the gods, chained the rebellious titan Prometheus to a mountaintop there. Georgia had enjoyed a golden age in the 1100s. Soon after, however, it was conquered by Genghis Khan's Mongols, and later

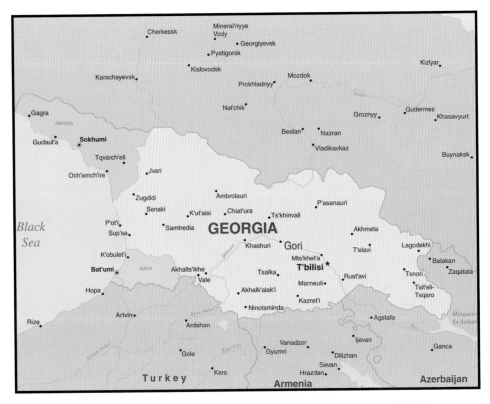

Stalin's homeland of Georgia became part of the United Soviet Socialist Republics not long after the Bolshevik Revolution in 1917.

by the Persians and Turks. By the late 1700s, the Georgians faced another invasion, this time by the Islamic peoples to the south. The Georgians, being Christians, sought protection from Islamic invasion from the Russian Empire in 1783. It was a case of inviting the wolf into the parlor; it would be over two hundred years before Georgia regained its independence.

By time Stalin was born, most Georgians resented

their Russian rulers and resisted attempts by the Russians to impose their laws and culture. Georgian culture was very different from Russia's. The Georgian language is part of a small family of languages called Kartvelian and, according to many scholars, unrelated to any other spoken tongue. The alphabet is also unique to the region, and there are distinctive Georgian foods, folklore, and customs. Throughout the 1800s, bands of Georgian patriots, and even more bandits, occasionally emerged from mountain hideouts to skirmish against the Russian invaders. Most armed resistance ended around 1860, but more passive resistance to Russian laws and ways did not.

In 1874 or 1875, a Georgian shoemaker named Vissarion "Beso" Djugashvili married fifteen-year-old Ekaterina Gheladze. Both were the children of former serfs. The couple settled in Gori, a river town of about 8,000 people. They rented a two-room brick house near the edge of town, possibly sharing the home with Beso's business partner. Furnishings were basic—a bed with a straw mattress, a table and stools, a trunk, and a mirror. Ekaterina cooked in a fireplace in the cellar.

Their first two children, both boys, died in infancy. Then, on December 6, 1878, Ekaterina gave birth to a third son. He was baptized Joseph Vissarionovich Djugashvili and was called Soso, the common Georgian nickname for Joseph.

Details of Soso's early childhood are scarce. We do know he was born into a stormy household. Beso drank

The medieval fortress of Goristsikhe overlooks Stalin's hometown of Gori, located in the Kartli province of Georgia. The town was almost entirely destroyed by an earthquake in 1920. (Le Monde Illustré, 1867)

up what little money he made and abused his wife and son. One of Stalin's childhood friends, Joseph Iremashvili, recalled that Soso was often the target of an "undeserved dreadful beatings." At times Ekaterina physically fought Beso during his drunken rages. She apparently beat her son, too.

When Soso was young, Beso gave up his shoemaking business and took a factory job in Tiflis, the Georgian capital. Though he returned to Gori on occasion, he never stayed long. He probably died of drink soon after. According to Iremashvili, "The early death of the father made no impression upon the boy. In the man he was supposed to call father he lost nothing." Ekaterina set about raising her six-year-old son alone. She took in wash to earn money. Among those she worked for were the local Russian Orthodox priests.

Soso was wiry and dark haired, with distinctive honey-colored eyes. Around the age of five, he survived a case of smallpox that left him with a pockmarked face. Along the way he also lost the partial use of his left arm. He later recalled a childhood blood infection in his hand. "I don't know what saved me then," he told his sister-in-law, "my strong constitution or the ointment of a village quack." Others remembered that the injury was caused when a carriage careened into a crowd and hit him. Whatever happened, the left arm remained shorter and weaker than the right for the rest of his life.

Though she doted on her son, work kept Ekaterina from spending much time with Soso. He grew into what Georgians called a *kinto*—a street kid or a roughneck. A friend remembered:

> Soso's favorite game was *krivi*. There were two teams of boxers: One drawn from those who lived in the upper town, the other representing the lower town. We pummeled each other unmercifully, and weedy little Soso was one of the craftiest scrappers. He had the knack of popping up unexpectedly behind a stronger opponent. But the well-fed children from the lower town were always stronger.

In Gori, the children of poor parents were usually apprenticed to older workers to learn a trade. The deeply

Joseph Vissarionovich Djugashvili at age sixteen. (Getty Images)

religious Ekaterina dreamed of Soso becoming a priest and was determined that he would get an education. She enrolled him at Gori's religious elementary school in 1888. She took whatever work she could get—house-cleaning, sewing, and laundry—to pay the tuition.

The school was strict. Students had to sit completely still. Looking away from the teacher for any reason meant a rod across the knuckles. Worse for Soso, the school authorities used education as a way to impose Russian values on the students. Teachers taught almost all of the classes in Russian. Soso, like many of the students, spoke only Georgian. The teachers encour-aged their pupils to speak Russian, using fists, rods, or orders to kneel on pebbles for an hour at a time.

Soso rose to the challenge. Before he left the school he overcame the language gap. "He was always prepared for lessons—waiting to be called on," a former class-mate said. "During class periods he would strain not to miss a single word or idea. He was all attention." The headmaster at Gori and a local priest arranged a schol-arship for him to study at the Russian Orthodox Semi-nary at Tiflis, the most important high school in the Caucasus. Ekaterina's wish for Soso to become a priest seemed to be coming true.

Soso arrived at the seminary at a tense time. For years there had been conflict between the non-Russian stu-dent body and the Russian monks in charge. In 1886, authorities had closed the school for several months following the murder of the Russian principal. The year before, students went on strike to insist on classes in Georgian literature, among other demands.

The clashes reflected changes in the ways the Russian government acted toward the non-Russian parts of the empire. The late 1800s brought new attempts to "Russify" the empire in hopes of tying resentful non-Russian citizens—Georgians, Poles, Finns, and others—more closely to the empire. The czarist government often enacted programs in inconsistent, ineffective ways, however, and the inept Russification program mostly angered non-Russians and actually sparked a renewal of nationalistic feelings, especially in young people.

The Tiflis Seminary, one of the training grounds for Georgia's brightest young men, became a hotbed of Georgian patriotism. Most of its six hundred students attended because it offered the country's best education, not because they wished to join the priesthood or become better Russians. The challenging curriculum offered classes in theology and Scripture, mathematics, history, and study in Greek and Latin. Students endured a highly structured day of prayer, classes, study, meager meals, and more prayer. The adult Stalin gave the seminary credit for pushing him onto his life's path:

> In protesting against the humiliating regime and the [J]esuitical methods that prevailed in the seminary, I was ready to become, and eventually did become, a revolutionary. . . . [T]he basis of all their methods is spying, prying, peering into people's souls, to subject

them to petty torment. What is there good in that? For instance, spying in the dormitory. At nine o'clock the bell rings for tea, we go to the dining hall, and when we return we find that a search has been made and all our boxes have been turned inside out. . . . What is there good in that?

Soso became sullen and quiet, and took to hiding away with books. He was considered to be a "touchy character," who responded even to good-natured jokes with a challenge to fight. In debate he bullied others, and when he lost he pouted and held grudges.

Soso managed to check out unapproved books from a local lending library. He fell in love with Russian and European authors such as Anton Chekhov and Victor Hugo. Economics and sociology also interested him, as did Charles Darwin's works on evolution. "We would sometimes read in the chapel during service, hiding the book under the pews," said G. Glurdjidze, another seminarian. "Of course we had to be extremely careful not to be caught by the masters. Books were Joseph's inseparable friends; he would not part with them even at meal times."

Soso's favorite book was a Georgian novel called *The Patricide*. Based in part on true events, *The Patricide* was the story of an outlaw named Koba and the fearful vengeance he takes on the Russians and the traitorous Georgians who help them oppress his country. Though simplistic, even crude, the novel had a huge effect on

Soso. "Koba had become his god, the sense of his life," Iremashvili said. "He wanted to become another Koba, as famous a fighter and hero: the figure of Koba was to be resurrected in him."

Books weren't the only source of forbidden ideas. Secret study groups met to discuss Georgian patriotism and other topics. As time passed, the talk turned to revolution. Revolutionary movements had a long history in Russia. These radical ideas covered a wide spectrum of beliefs, from the Anarchists, believers in a society without government, to the Tolstoyans, believers in universal brotherhood, to the *Narodniks* and their determination to turn Russia's enormous peasant population into a revolutionary force for change. During the last years of the nineteenth century, a new kind of revolutionary began to turn up in Tiflis: the Marxists.

Karl Marx was a German philosopher, born in 1818, who believed philosophy should be used to change the world. The theory of Marxism, which was developed in works Marx wrote himself and with the Englishman Frederick Engels (1820-1895), was a reaction to the misery brought on by the Industrial Revolution. Marx believed the working class, which he dubbed the proletariat, was a new type of human being that could change the world from the bottom up, *if* it realized it had the power to do so. It was a radical idea for the 1800s, when society and many religions taught that God intended for some to rule and some to serve; for an individual to defy his assigned role was to defy God.

Karl Marx's critique of capitalism and articulation of class struggle formed the basis for much of Soviet ideology in the twentieth century. (Library of Congress)

Marx believed society could not be equal for everyone as long as the capitalists who owned the factories, land, and other profitable parts of the economy—which made up the class he called the bourgeoisie—profited from the proletariat's labor. The bourgeoisie, he said, had no interest in improving the lives of most of their workers. They would become richer and richer, while the proletariat fell further and further behind. This would never change unless the working class organized into a political force and seized power.

Marx and Engels laid out a simplified version of their idea in the *Communist Manifesto,* published in 1848. Only the working class could free itself, they thundered, but first it had to recognize that it was locked into constant conflict with the bourgeoisie. "Workers of the world, unite!," were the first words of the *Communist Manifesto.* Workers throughout the industrial world had to join together to seize power.

In Marx's prediction of the future, workers would eventually come to power and would confiscate the bourgeoisie's wealth. The worker's governments could then abolish land ownership and other forms of private property. All land and what was called the means of production would be owned by the state. The economy, including food production, would be planned by the state. There would be free public education and other public services, such as health and assistance to the aged and infirm.

Marx warned that creating a Communist utopia would be a long and bitter struggle. The more the working class advanced, the more the bourgeoisie would resist. The capitalists would use every resource—including the army and police—to keep the proletariat powerless. The conflict would inevitably become violent and the proletariat would have to fight a revolution to overthrow capitalism. With that achieved, society would enter its final phase of development, the establishment of communism, a fairer, more highly evolved system that would take care of and value every human.

Marx's ideas were a more radical and systematic version of the socialistic ideas that were current in Europe at the time and only gained adherents slowly, mostly among intellectuals. When Soso came across them fifty years after the *Communist Manifesto* had been published, only a tiny number of Russians—and fewer Georgians—had much interest in Marxism. But during his time at the seminary, the ideas slowly seeped into disaffected parts of Russian society.

Soso began to spend more time off-campus with seasoned radicals, many of them ex-seminarians. Influenced by Marx, who said religion was merely a tool to keep the majority of the people compliant, he became an atheist—although he was still, at least nominally, studying for the priesthood. In time he joined the local Marxist group, the Social Democrats. Before long, amidst clouds of tobacco smoke, Soso was lecturing shoemakers, printers, and railway workers on the basics of Marxism. He probably found a receptive audience. Many Georgians endured horrible working conditions and little pay.

Having committed to radical politics, it was logical that Soso leave the seminary. But revolutionary work did not pay, and he lacked job skills. If he could finish his last year, a seminary degree would open the door to a university education. But on May 29, 1899, the seminary expelled him for skipping his final exams.

For much of the rest of the year, he scraped together money from tutoring and through the generosity of seminary friends. At the end of the year, Lado Ketskhoveli, one of Soso's Social Democrat mentors, got him a clerk's job at the local observatory. "We had to keep awake all night," Ketskhoveli said, "and make observations at stated intervals with the help of intricate instruments. The work demanded great nervous concentration and patience." The pay was low, but there was a free room. Soon, however, Soso gave up the job. This was the only everyday job he ever held.

Although Marxism was atheistic, it was not an altogether strange choice for an ex-seminarian. In some ways it even appealed to the Christian ideals Soso learned at the Tiflis school. Marxism, like parts of the Bible, romanticized the poor and the suffering. After the Marxist revolution, the meek would inherit the earth, and those who hungered for righteousness would form a human society based on equality, compassion, and respect for humanity. Marxism, like the Russian Orthodox Church, demanded unquestioning faith. Stalin's daughter Svetlana later said, "This lack of compromise, this inflexibility, this inability to agree with an opposing opinion even if it was obviously a good one, I also attribute to his experiences at the seminary, where students had been imbued with fanaticism and intolerance."

Two
WHAT IS TO
BE DONE?

Stalin, who soon assumed the alias Koba, joined the underground at a time when young people across the empire were gravitating toward radical politics. The various movements drew members from all nationalities, both genders, and all classes. But revolutionary parties drew in particular from the *intelligentsia*—civil servants, academics, and educated professionals (lawyers, doctors, journalists, teachers, and the like). Few, however, came from working class or peasant backgrounds. In this way Soso, the son of a poor shoemaker, was unusual.

Stalin devoted himself to being a practical—doing the unglamorous hands-on work to build a Marxist movement. He learned how to be a printer and set up a secret printing press that provided a vital link in the communications between Marxist intellectuals living in Europe and the rank and file inside Russia.

Revolutionaries lived rough lives, constantly broke and often hungry. "I visited Koba several times in his wretched little room," Iremashvili recalled. "He would be wearing a black Russian blouse with the red tie so typical of Social Democrats. You never saw him in anything but that dirty blouse and unpolished shoes."

Stalin was arrested for revolutionary activities for the first time in April 1902 and spent eighteen months in local prisons before being sent to Siberia for the first time.

In the old days political prisoners walked into exile in chains. But in Stalin's era the authorities treated political prisoners with a lighter hand. Trains, boats, and carts were the usual modes of transportation. Revolutionaries considered exile a rite of passage. Sent to remote areas, left with time on their hands, they passed the days studying and writing and debating, often with veteran revolutionaries as their teachers. The Siberian authorities tended to be lenient, even indifferent. Often exiles could send for their wives or mothers to come stay with them. They received government money for necessities; if jobs were available, they could work. When it came time to escape, and escape was another rite of passage, a political prisoner bribed a local to carry him via cart or reindeer-sled to transportation on the railroad or a major river. Often it was just a matter of being

Stalin, in 1902, during his first exile. (Getty Images)

smuggled enough cash and a set of "boots," the underground slang for forged identity papers.

Stalin's boots arrived sometime before early 1904. By February, he was back in Tiflis. Two major events had taken place in his absence. First, his friend Ketskhoveli was dead—shot in jail the previous August. But it was the second event that had a far greater impact on his life.

In July 1903, a group of Russian Marxists met in a flea-infested room in Brussels, and then again in London, to form a single Social Democratic party, the Russian Social Democratic Workers Party (RSDWP). It is often said that revolutionaries need arguments like most people need oxygen, and the Russians were no exception. The conference delegates bickered so much over ideas and tactics that the RSDWP threatened to fall apart as soon as it had been founded. The figure at the center of many arguments was the ex-lawyer named Vladimir Ilyich Lenin.

Lenin, who was born on April 22, 1870, grew up in a solid Russian middle-class family. His father was an inspector of schools, and the family stressed education. Lenin was probably set on the revolutionary path as a teenager when his beloved older brother was executed for conspiring in a failed attempt to assassinate Czar Alexander III.

Lenin began his studies at the university at Kazan in the fall of 1887. In December, he attended a demonstration, for which he was arrested and expelled from school. For the next few years, authorities refused to let him return, nor would they allow him to pursue an education abroad. Only after years of rejections did he receive permission to take the tests to become a lawyer. In November 1891, he received a diploma with honors but soon gave up the law for radical politics. Over the next ten years, Lenin emerged as a major revolutionary figure, brilliant and energetic but equally stubborn and fanatical in defense of his ideas. A political rival observed: "There is no other man who is absorbed by the revolution twenty-four hours a day, who has no other thoughts but the thought of revolution, and who, even when he sleeps, dreams of nothing but revolution."

At the time of the Brussels-London congress, Lenin led one of several factions inside the larger organization of Russian Social Democrats. Each faction had its own ideas and priorities, but many members agreed the movement needed to recruit more people. With other

Vladimir Ilyich Lenin.
(Library of Congress)

European Social Democratic parties gaining influence in their countries, particularly in Germany, some Russian Social Democrats thought it time to create a mass movement in the spirit of Marx's idea that workers must form their own unions and parties to transform the political system.

Lenin vehemently argued against a large, mass-based party. The year before, he had published *What Is To Be Done?*, which argued that only a small, disciplined group of professional revolutionaries could lead a successful Marxist revolution. *What Is To Be Done?* reinterpreted Marx's original ideas and boldly rejected the idea of a mass revolution by ordinary people. Power, Lenin said, sould be seized by a disciplined few that would hold it until the workers were ready to rule on their own.

The conference ended with the Social Democrats divided into two major factions. Though Lenin's side was smaller, he cleverly took the name *Bolsheviks* (majority), leaving the real majority with the label of *Mensheviks* (minority). Over the next thirteen years, until the Russian Revolution, the views of both sides evolved. In general, the Mensheviks tended to be more moderate and favored participating in elections, while the Bolsheviks insisted on small numbers and high discipline, though in time they came around to taking part in elections and similar tactics.

By the time Stalin returned from Siberian exile, the Mensheviks dominated Georgia's Social Democrats. He sided with the Bolsheviks. "He worshipped Lenin, he deified Lenin," one revolutionary said. "He lived on Lenin's thoughts, copied him so closely that we jokingly called him 'Lenin's left leg.'" It was no surprise the ideas in *What Is To Be Done?* appealed to Stalin. It was a handbook for practical workers like him, and at the same time a call for revolutionary heroes to step up and lead the way. His attitude toward Lenin would change somewhat when he actually met him and discovered that he was a mere mortal, but the power of his arguments had made him a disciple.

By 1905, Russia was on the precipice. Controlled by one of the last absolute monarchs in Europe, the vast land mass, filled with different nationalities and ethnic groups, was coming apart at the seams. The new century was proving to be too much for a nation hobbled by political corruption and inefficiency, a weak educational system, and stifling bureaucracy. Beginning with Czar Peter the Great (1672-1725), there had been attempts made at modernization, and over the last decades of the nineteenth century, industrial development had quickened. But the current czar, Nicholas II, was uninspiring and ineffective at meeting either the internal problems or the pressures presented by the increasingly threatening outside world.

Even the industrial growth that had occurred had created social strains as peasants flooded into the cities looking for jobs. The sudden population shift created overcrowded city slums. Workers, increasingly angry at their poor pay and unhealthy living and working

Europe, including western Russia and part of Siberia, in 1905. (Courtesy of the University of Texas Libraries, The University of Texas at Austin.)

conditions, became open to radical new ideas that promised to improve their lives. In the countryside, the frustrated peasants wanted the same thing and believed the fields belonging to their landlords could provide it.

Although the czar's secret police struggled to stamp out dissent, criticism of the czarist system came from all levels of society—professionals and intellectuals, as well as workers and students. Even a smattering of noblemen and millionaires were sympathetic and gave money to revolutionary groups. Most frightening of all was a series of assassinations carried out by anarchists and other radicals, who were usually from non-Marxist

revolutionary groups that idealized the peasants and believed they and their dream of more land had to be the heart of any future revolution in Russia.

Nicholas II tried halfheartedly to respond to the growing unrest. He preferred the advice of his favorite noblemen or ministers, who agreed with him. Most of all he listened to his wife Alexandra, a German princess known for her narrow-minded political views and obsession with religious mysticism. Wiser heads managed to rise to high positions occasionally. One of the leading figures at the turn of the century was Count Sergei Witte, a promoter of industrialization and the mastermind of the Trans-Siberian Railroad linking European Russia with Asia. But ministers smarter or more gifted than Nicholas seldom lasted long in his service.

Sometime around 1903 or 1904, Nicholas's conservative advisors and representatives of various business interests proposed that a short, victorious war with Japan would solve all the czar's problems. Japan was considered a rising power in the Far East and an obstacle to Russia's plans to expand its influence in that direction. The war, the thinking went, would defeat Japan's economic ambitions while at the same time generating a surge of patriotism to calm the unrest inside Russia. Witte, among others, disagreed. But in Nicholas's circle no one believed that a country of mere "Asiatics"—an obviously inferior people in their minds—had a chance against mighty Russia.

Opposite: *Nicholas II, the last czar of Russia.* (Tsarskoe Selo Museum-Preserve)

In the end, Japan made the czar's decision for him. On February 8, 1904, the Japanese navy attacked Russia's naval base at Port Arthur, Manchuria. The dreamed-of short, victorious war quickly turned into a disaster for the Russians. The numerically superior Russian army—poorly supplied, badly led, and made up of peasant recruits—suffered ghastly casualties. In January 1905, Port Arthur fell after a long siege. But the most stunning defeat came in the naval battle at Tsushima Strait on May 27-28, when Japan destroyed Russia's Baltic Fleet, which had sailed halfway around the world, in a matter of hours.

Frustration over the government's incompetent handling of the war soured the public on the whole adventure. Soon the frustration boiled over. Nicholas made a few reluctant compromises on land reform and other pressing social issues, which only raised the reformers' hopes. The situation in the winter of 1905 was primed for explosion.

In January 1905, as the fall of Port Arthur became inevitable, the workers of St. Petersburg prepared to march on the czar's Winter Palace. The march's main organizer was a priest named Father George Gapon. He hoped to lead a peaceful demonstration to present a list of workers' complaints to Nicholas. Gapon was not a radical. He refused to allow revolutionary parties to take part, and the demonstrators carried portraits of the czar and sang patriotic songs in Nicholas's honor. As the crowd neared the Winter Palace, however, soldiers ordered them to disperse. When they refused, shots were

Imperial guards fire on unarmed demonstrators during what came to be known as Russia's "Bloody Sunday." (Central Revolutionary Museum, Moscow)

fired into the crowd and mounted Cossack troops charged forward. At least two hundred people died. Eight hundred or more were hurt.

Outrage at the massacre swept the country, and strikes and peasant revolts broke out. Workers in St. Petersburg began to elect councils, called *soviets*, to exercise power on their behalf. A desperate Nicholas returned Witte to power. On Witte's advice, the czar reluctantly agreed to reforms. They released a manifesto that promised civil liberties and voting rights for many, but not all, to elect a parliament, called a Duma. The manifesto appeared to be a victory for moderate reform, and as Witte intended, it headed off extreme revolutionary feelings.

Once order was restored, though, Nicholas refused to honor the spirit of the promises he had made. Nicholas ignored the Duma and appointed the ruthless Peter Stolypin to govern the country as his premier. Stolypin dissolved the Duma and cracked down on all opposition with such ferocity that Russians called the nooses used for hangings "Stolypin neckties." After holding new elections with restricted voting rights, the Duma was packed with representatives of the conservative upper classes. The 1905 revolution had failed.

Stalin, like the Social Democrats as a whole, played a small role in the Revolution of 1905. Lenin had stated that a spontaneous revolt without disciplined revolutionary leadership was doomed to failure, and in the end events seemed to prove him right. However, when the Social Democrats gathered in Tammerfors, Finland, for their 1905 conference, which was held before the Stolypin reaction began, Lenin and other Social Democrats were optimistic that czardom's days were numbered.

When Stalin arrived, he found the conference's main goal was the reunification of the Bolsheviks and Mensheviks. People on both sides felt the split weakened the Social Democrats, and the two sides did reach tentative agreement. In the meantime, there was debate on whether to run candidates for the Duma. Lenin, surprisingly, leaned toward the Menshevik's position that the Duma offered a high-profile place to preach revolution. But many hardcore Bolsheviks, Stalin included, argued that participation in the Duma would be a sellout to czardom. Lenin eventually agreed to go along with them.

This was Stalin's first time meeting Lenin, and he returned to Tiflis unimpressed with the physical appearance of the Bolshevik leader:

> I had hoped to see the mountain eagle of our party, the great man, great physically as well as politically. I had fancied Lenin as a giant, stately and imposing. How great was my disappointment to see a most ordinary-looking man, below average height, in no way, literally in no way, distinguishable from ordinary mortals.

The next year Stalin took his first trip out of the Russian Empire when he traveled to the Social Democrat conference in Stockholm, Sweden. By then the mood for unification had passed. The Mensheviks had resumed their more moderate positions, to the disgust of some Bolsheviks, and the conference fell into familiar arguments. One of the more bitter controversies concerned the practical question of how the party should raise money for expenses. This debate affected Stalin personally.

After the failure of the Revolution of 1905, donations to the Social Democrats from their rich sympathizers and the intelligentsia dried up. Squads of revolutionaries, sometimes allied with conventional criminals, had taken to raising funds by robbing banks, mail coaches, and steamships, and referrung to them as expropriations.

As it turned out, an unusually high number of these robberies took place in and around Georgia. Many worried that such blatant criminal activity would ruin the party's reputation. After a debate, and over Lenin's loud opposition, the conference banned further expropriations.

The vote did not stop the practice, however. Those involved simply hid the "exes," as the expropriated money was called, from the rest of the party. Some suspected Stalin of being one of the ringleaders of the robberies. His part in the crimes, as well as Lenin's, remains unclear. According to some historians he helped plan jobs rather than carry them out, but his main role may have been to get the money to party leaders living in Europe. Whatever the facts, the number of exes spiked after the Stockholm conference. A deadly raid on June 26, 1907, in Tiflis made headlines across Europe. The assailants lobbed bombs into a crowded square as carriages filled with money passed by. Several soldiers, policemen, and bystanders were killed. It soon became known that Social Democrats had organized the robbery. The Mensheviks condemned the crime, but the damage to the party's reputation was done.

Stalin's next few years were a blur of underground activity, prison cells, and Siberian exile. Sometime along the way he got married, perhaps in 1905 or 1906. Remarkably, the atheist agreed to a church ceremony at his wife's request. His new wife, Ekaterina Svanidze, was a seamstress and the sister of a local revolutionary. For a time, the poverty-stricken couple kept a shack near the

Baku oil fields, where Stalin was organizing workers. In 1907, Ekaterina gave birth to a son named Yakov. Sometime later, she became seriously ill. Lacking money to pay a doctor, Stalin may have moved her to the Tiflis area, where her family could look after her. He was in jail when she died. The authorities let him out to attend the funeral. Iremashvili, his old seminary companion, showed up to pay his respects. That Iremashvili was now a Menshevik did not, for once, matter to Stalin. Iremashvili remembered: "Koba firmly pressed my hand, pointed to the coffin, and said, 'This creature softened my heart of stone. She died and with her died my last warm feelings for people.' He placed his right hand on his chest. 'It is all so desolate here inside, so inexpressibly empty.'"

In late March 1908, authorities charged Stalin with leading an underground organization. He was sent to two years' exile in central Siberia.

After the heady days of 1905, the Social Democratic movement had hit rock bottom. The government crackdown had taken a toll. Police harassment, the cold and solitude of Siberian exile, the constant worries about police spies and double-crossers—it was a hard life, and unbearable if one lost hope of ever seeing a victorious revolution. Poverty-related illnesses, emotional breakdowns, and suicides took the lives of many revolutionaries; others mellowed with age and gave up the cause. Stalin, after another escape from Siberia, stopped in St. Petersburg and found that the

Social Democrats there numbered only three hundred members. There had once been thousands.

After his sentence was up in June 1911, Stalin was forbidden to settle in a large city. He chose to live in Vologda, a popular destination for exiles northeast of Moscow. Sergo Ordzhonikidze, another Georgian Bolshevik, visited him there in February 1912 and brought stunning news. The Bolsheviks had broken for good from the Mensheviks, and Lenin had selected Stalin for his new Bolshevik party's leadership council, the Central Committee. It was an unexpected honor for a relative unknown, but Lenin had tired of intellectuals. He wanted to surround himself with practicals, especially those loyal to him, and he liked Stalin's toughness and loyalty.

Stalin escaped Vologda at the end of February. Back in St. Petersburg, he supervised a new Bolshevik paper called *Pravda* (Truth). It was an influential position, but also one that Lenin watched closely. Like others of Lenin's collaborators, Stalin eventually found himself in trouble with the Bolshevik leader when he toned down Lenin's attacks on the Mensheviks in *Pravda*. Lenin, furious at being edited, replaced Stalin and summoned the Bolshevik leaders to his home in Krakow, then a city in the Austro-Hungarian Empire, to make clear what he expected from them.

Angering Lenin was risky. He demanded discipline and total allegiance. But Lenin also studied his followers, their weaknesses and strengths, what they could offer to his movement, the ways to motivate as well as discipline them. He devoted time to building the skills and reputations of certain Bolsheviks. The stronger each person, he said, the stronger the movement. He decided the best way to strengthen Stalin was to send him to Vienna to research "Marxism and the National Question," a study of the non-Russian nationalities of the Russian Empire. The essay was published in an important Marxist journal, and later as a stand-alone booklet, under the byline K. Stalin (Man of Steel).

Once the essay was done, Stalin returned to Russia to take up new duties. On February 22, he attended a fundraising concert for *Pravda*. Okhrana agents, members of the secret police, tipped off about the concert and Stalin's presence there, surrounded the theater. Stalin's arrest was part of a nationwide sweep. To Lenin's shock, the entire Bolshevik leadership inside Russia vanished into the czar's prisons. When the sentences came down, Stalin received his most severe punishment yet—four years in the wilderness of northern Siberia.

Three
From Exile to
Revolution

In middle of 1913, Stalin arrived in the Turukhansk territory of central Siberia. By tradition, exiled revolutionaries greeted a new arrival with food, drink, and a place to stay. By the same tradition, the newcomer filled in his comrades on the latest news from Russia and abroad. To the surprise of Turukhansk's exile community, however, Stalin immediately closed the door to his room when he arrived. He clearly had no interest in discussing news or celebrating his arrival.

Early the next year, the secret police heard of plans to get money and "boots" to Stalin for an escape. The tip came from Roman Malinovsky, a charismatic leader of the Bolsheviks—and one of the Okhrana's most prized spies. Malinovsky was the informant who had betrayed

Stalin to the police to begin with. Lenin, however, had total trust in him and had assigned Malinovsky the job of getting Stalin cash and ID papers. To prevent any chance of escape, the police moved Stalin and a second Bolshevik, Yakov Sverdlov, to Kureika, a remote village above the Arctic Circle.

Sverdlov was the Bolsheviks' most talented organizer and, like his roommate, a member of the Central Committee inside Russia. "With me is the Georgian, Djugashvili, an old acquaintance whom I already know from another exile," Sverdlov wrote in a letter. "A good fellow, but too much of an individualist in everyday life."

Sverdlov and Stalin had shared an unhappy time together during a previous exile, where Stalin had often tricked his tidy roommate into doing all the housework. In Kureika, it took all of two months for Stalin to wear out his reputation as a good fellow. Sverdlov moved out, explaining, "We know each other very well. And the saddest thing is that in conditions of exile or prison a man is stripped bare before you and revealed in all petty respects. . . . Now the comrade and I are living in different quarters and rarely see each other." This was in a town of fifty people, where Stalin and Sverdlov were the only political prisoners.

Stalin spent most of his time alone. He read from a library he had stolen from a deceased comrade and wrote letters. A few of his more desperate notes asked Malinovsky, the Okhrana spy, for aid. Stalin even begged help from Georgia's Mensheviks, the same people he had attacked for years.

Stalin was now in his mid-thirties—looking at least ten years older—and for all his adult life he had lived in poverty, on the run from the police or in prison or exile. He had nothing to show for his sacrifices except a police file too lengthy to ever permit him to return to normal life, if he was inclined to do so. And now, just as he had earned recognition within the small Bolshevik community, he had been shipped to the edge of the civilized world. Perhaps his time in Kureika intensified the harder parts of his personality—his ruthlessness, his misanthropy, his fear of being forgotten within the

From 1912, a card from the register of the St. Petersburg imperial police on Joseph Stalin. (Courtesy of Getty Images.)

Bolshevik movement. Perhaps the bitterness of living such a difficult life transformed his idealism about the revolution into the hunger for power that served him so well in the future.

World War I, which began in August 1914, provided Stalin an escape from the Arctic. The government began calling up political prisoners to serve in the army. Stalin traveled via dogsled, reindeer-sleigh, and on foot to take the required physical. His injured left arm kept him out of the service, but he soon got a second break. The authorities let him serve out the rest of his time in Achinsk, a town on the Trans-Siberian Railroad. There he was able to reestablish ties with the Social Democratic movement. He remained in Achinsk until 1917.

Achinsk's community of Bolshevik exiles revolved around the house of Lev Kamenev, a writer and one of Lenin's oldest associates. Kamenev looked like a painting of a radical intellectual, with his somber face, spectacles, and well-groomed pointy beard. Mild-mannered, he tended toward moderate behavior, though he was known for stubbornly defending his ideas, even to Lenin. He was born Lev Borisovich Rosenfeld in 1883, the son of a railroad engineer. After being thrown out of law school, Kamenev met Lenin in Paris and soon after became a Bolshevik. Though he had an on-again, off-again relationship with the Bolshevik leader—he wanted to reunify with the Mensheviks, among other disputes— Kamenev was undeniably an insider. He had taken a turn as *Pravda* editor after Stalin's arrest. After the outbreak of war, he was arrested along with the Bolshevik Duma representatives and sent to Siberia.

Russia, like all the countries of Europe, went to war with enthusiasm. This enthusiasm was motivated by two strategic goals that had lived in the heart of the ruling class for decades. The first concerned control of the Dardanelles, the vital sea route that connected the Black Sea to the Mediterranean. The aging Ottoman Empire controlled the straits, but it was near collapse. Russian strategists saw an excellent opportunity to fulfill the age-old dream of expanding south for economic and military gain.

The second dream concerned Russia's longing for hegemony, or dominant authority, in southeastern Europe. Already the site of a series of minor wars—involving Serbia, Montenegro, Greece, Bulgaria, and the Ottoman Turks—the Balkans were a playing field where Russian-backed Slavic peoples, principally the Serbs, competed against Austria-Hungary and the Turks. Germany, France, and Great Britain had interfered in the Balkans for reasons of their own, and the hope was that the war would leave Russia unhindered in what it considered to be its sphere of influence.

The czar's wiser advisors worried that the conflict would push czarism to the brink. Peter Durnovo, a former Minister of the Interior, warned Nicholas of "social revolution in its most extreme form" if the war went against Russia. He predicted the public would blame the czar's government for defeats and that massive desertions would drain the army's ability to fight. Russia, he

said, "will be thrown into total anarchy, the consequences of which cannot even be foreseen."

Nicholas ignored the advice. On a military level,
Russia went to war better prepared than it had in 1905,
though too much of Russian military thinking relied on
a perceived inexhaustible supply of soldiers, rather than
on modern weapons and strategy. Even so, in the beginning Russia matched up reasonably well with the de-
crepit Austro-Hungarian Empire.

Germany was a different matter. German industrial
might dominated Europe; its army was one of the best
in the world. These factors prepared the country for what
became the first modern, total war, leaving behind the
old, fading empires, such as Austria-Hungary and Russia.

It did not take long for the collapse to begin. Bloody
battles in the first months of the war decimated Russia's
best-trained and most loyal and motivated officers.
Russian industry could not replace the ammunition,
artillery shells, food, clothing, or other material used by
the military. About all that could be replaced was man-
power, in the form of millions of peasant recruits. In the
short run this impressive mass of bodies made it the
largest army in the war. In the long run it was a disaster.

The pressure of the terrible war splintered the al-
ready-fractured Russian society and political system.
Soldiers were dying by the thousands fighting to protect
a political system that did little to make their lives better
or hold out the promise of more freedoms. By 1917,
large numbers of them had ceased to believe in their

government or the once beloved czar. Peasant soldiers had no idea why they fought. Uneducated and nonpolitical, their idea of themselves as Russians—as members of a large nation—was weak. Their allegiance was to their home villages and their farms. This attitude alone caused a morale problem and, combined with other factors, such as shortages of food, weapons, and other essentials, left the Russian soldier at the mercy of the better-trained, better-supplied Germans. Their lives seemed to have no value. Uncaring officers ordered them to run at enemy trenches with nothing but a bayonet or sent them into battle unarmed, with orders to take the rifles of the dead. At one time, supplies were so low that Russian commanders considered arming the troops with hatchets at the ends of poles—to fight against a German army equipped with machine guns and artillery. As Durnovo had predicted, wartime strains created a political crisis behind the lines. And as in 1905, the czar's inability to govern presented a critical problem.

In 1915, Nicholas left Petrograd altogether to take command at the front. The gesture was intended to rally the troops. It also relieved him of the burden of politics, something that had worn him down. But his departure left a power vacuum in the city. To the dismay of many, including some who loved the czar, Alexandra stepped into the gap created by her husband's absence. Her very background was a public relations disaster. Here was a German princess exercising enormous power in a nation at war with Germany. People began to whisper rumors

ST. PETERSBURG

Located on the Gulf of Finland in northwest Russia, St. Petersburg was named for its founder, Czar Peter the Great, in 1703. The city was a convenient port and gateway to Europe, and served as Russia's capital until 1918 (when the capital was moved to Moscow). Home today to nearly five million people, St. Petersburg is Russia's second-largest city. It is home to many historic buildings, monuments, palaces, and churches.

In 1914, at the outbreak of World War I, the city was renamed Petrograd in order to sound less German. Ten years later, the city was again renamed, this time Leningrad, in honor of the former Soviet leader.

Finally, in 1991, with the end of the Soviet Union, just over 50 percent of its citizens voted to restore St. Petersburg's original name.

St. Petersburg at the turn of the century. (Library of Congress)

that she and her advisors worked against Russian interests. In addition, the czarina's high-strung personality poorly suited her for decision making at times of crisis. She took advice from a group of yes-men and corrupt officials, and from the mysterious mystic Rasputin, a monk with hypnotic eyes and a supposed ability to alleviate her son Alexei's hemophilia. Even the most patriotic, hardworking officials found it difficult to get things done in such a system.

Russians of all political beliefs began to consider possible alternatives to the autocracy. The political parties had their own positions on the war. The Kadets, the liberal reform party and the most powerful group in the Duma, voted overwhelmingly to remain in the conflict. There were many opinions among the pro-peasant Socialist Revolutionaries, one of the least cohesive parties, but in general they agreed that Germany had to be defeated to prevent its conservative government from dominating European politics. Most Mensheviks took a solid antiwar position that argued for an immediate peace, with all sides giving up its claims.

The Bolsheviks took the most controversial position. As a Marxist, Lenin considered war between nations as a last gasp of the capitalist system. He argued that capitalism made war inevitable. "War is not an accident, not a 'sin,'" he wrote in 1914, ". . . but an unavoidable stage of capitalism, just as normal a form of capitalist life as is peace." To destroy capitalism for good, the revolution had to pound a stake through its heart.

Only that kind of bold action could make the world safe for communism. Since it was the struggle between the social classes that mattered to the workers, he urged soldiers, who were also workers, of all nations to turn their weapons away from each other and instead point them at the governments that oppressed them.

However, the Bolsheviks could do little in the way of bold action. Their leadership was trapped in various European countries or in Siberian exile. Most Russians looking for an alternative to the czar put their hopes in the Duma. Though it currently lacked power, Russia's parliament was an existing political institution. The Kadets saw the situation as a chance to reform Russia's political system by transforming an out-of-date monarchy into something closer to the twentieth-century democratic systems of Western Europe.

The Kadets' fear was that the war situation was deteriorating so fast a Marxist revolution might sweep them aside along with the czar. Soldiers were deserting the army by the thousands. Behind the front lines, workers and other civilians in the cities found it harder to get basic necessities, including food. Although the peasants were growing enough food, they refused to sell it to the government at artificially low prices. The Kadets realized the Bolsheviks were beginning to find unhappy people willing to listen to them.

The Kadets, frightened by the atmosphere, toned down their criticisms of the czar's government, in hopes of easing him out. "[T]he strain is so great that any carelessly thrown match may kindle a terrible fire," said one Kadet leader. "This would be not a revolution but a terrible Russian riot, senseless and pitiless. It would be an orgy of the mob."

But Nicholas refused to listen to warnings. On one occasion, a well-meaning visitor begged him to take action, but the czar snapped, "Hurry up and finish [your report]. I can't waste time on this. . . . I already know everything that I need to know, and your information simply contradicts mine." He further alienated the Kadets by appointing a dictator to rule in his name.

In the end, it was the Russian people—hungry, unhappy, sick of war and a government unable to lead—that overthrew the czar. The so-called February Revolution began in Petrograd. In late February 1917, strikes spread throughout the capital city. The authorities managed to restore order for a short time, but the situation remained fluid. At first the Bolsheviks considered the demonstrations nothing more than a *golodnyi bunt*, a riot for food. "What revolution?" exclaimed one leader of Petrograd's Bolsheviks. "Give the workers a loaf of bread and the movement will peter out."

The 1905 revolution had failed in large part because the army remained behind the czar. In 1917, tens of thousands of unhappy peasant soldiers garrisoned in Petrograd resented the orders to fire on unarmed demonstrators and began to mutiny. By the evening of February 27, Petrograd's commander had, at most, 2,000 loyal troops.

In Petrograd on February 27, 1917, workers and peasants gather in mutiny against the czar. (Courtesy of Art Resource.)

Nicholas's advisors began to pressure him to abdicate. By handing power to the Duma, he could give the demonstrators the change of government they demanded. Better to put Russia's fate in the hands of the moderate Kadets, the advisors said, than to risk a rise to power by the likes of the Bolsheviks and Mensheviks. But now the Kadets, caught by surprise, hesitated to take power. For all they knew, the Petrograd protests might evaporate at any moment. If Nicholas got the upper hand again, as he had in 1905, they could face treason charges and execution. The Duma hedged its bets by declaring itself a temporary provisional government. Nicholas abdicated on March 2, and the Romanov dynasty, in power for over three hundred years, came to an end.

Throughout the country the traditional institutions of authority and law and order just melted away. Groups of workers searched the homes of former czarist officials, locked up many, murdered a few, and often requisitioned their belongings. The 1905 soviets, councils of workers, reorganized in the factories and began to take control from the owners. In the countryside, the peasants began to claim the land of the hated landlords as their own. The provisional government made an idealistic declaration in favor of civil liberties and power for local governments.

As the smoke cleared, it was obvious the country considered the Duma the heroes of the victory over czardom. The Bolsheviks had to figure out where they fit into the new system and where the events of the past few weeks fit into Marxist theory.

The new government ordered a general release of political prisoners, and the newly freed Stalin hurried to Petrograd. He stayed at the apartment of his old friend Sergei Alliluyev, a railroad worker and Bolshevik comrade he had known since his days in Georgia. Anna Alliluyeva, Sergei's daughter, remembered his appearance: "He was still wearing the same suit, the same Russian blouse and felt boots, but his face looked considerably older. He amused us with his impersonations of the orators who had organized receptions at the [train] stations."

Stalin was one of the first Bolshevik leaders to arrive. He and Kamenev took command of *Pravda*. No longer did they work in the cold back room of a slum building. Now they were headquartered in the mansion of a ballerina. For the next month, Stalin and Kamenev spent most of their time in the *Pravda* offices, while Lenin and the other leaders scrambled to get back to Russia. Stalin also accepted an invitation to join the leadership committee of the Petrograd Soviet (the ruling council of the city), a position that gave him a taste of real power for the first time.

The main issue facing all the political parties was whether to support the provisional government. Initially, based on the Marxist theory that a society had to have a bourgeois democracy before it could have a Socialist revolution, the Bolsheviks running *Pravda* followed the Menshevik's lead and gave their support. After all, the provisional government was not the immediate problem; a resurgence of czarist forces represented a far greater threat. Everyone knew conservative elements in society, and the military, had not given up the idea of retaking power. In order to protect against that possibility, the Bolsheviks and Men-sheviks tried again to unify, with Stalin actively taking part.

As usual, talk of reconciliation angered Lenin. The Bolshevik leader remained stuck in Krakow, unable to cross the war zone on the eastern front, but via messenger he sent two "Letters from Afar" for immediate publication in *Pravda*. In them he argued that Russia was ready for a Socialist revolution and that the worker-controlled soviets nationwide must take power. Stalin and Kamenev, both loyal Bolsheviks, worried that their leader was being unrealistic. They edited out the more explosive sections of one letter before printing it. The other they refused to run at all.

Both men, having crossed Lenin in the past, knew the risk they were taking. Stalin's response to Lenin's letters revealed a trait that would reappear many times in the future. By pretending to be someone willing to compromise, he appeared as a reasonable person to both sides in a dispute, in this case between the hardcore Bolsheviks (his own faction) and the far more numerous Social Democrats of all kinds, who wanted a unified party. Like many clever politicians, he refused to take a side until he knew which way things would go. Then he backed the winning side, even if it meant going against his own past words and actions.

On April 3, Lenin arrived by train at the Finland Station in Petrograd. The German government had provided him a way home, hoping that his presence would further destabilize Russia. They even gave Lenin money for revolutionary activity.

Lenin immediately confronted Kamenev. "What's this you're writing in *Pravda*?" he said. He blasted the idea of unification with the Mensheviks and called for land to be taken from the rural landlords to be parceled out to the peasants. He demanded the provisional government give power over to the soviets, the true representatives of the working class. Non-Bolsheviks considered Lenin out of touch. Even Stalin and his comrades at *Pravda* granted that "Lenin's general scheme appears to us unacceptable."

With Lenin's return, Stalin faded into the background. During the summer of 1917, he returned to the grind of party work, passing along Bolshevik orders to its working-class followers and twisting arms to make sure Bolshevik members of the Petrograd Soviet voted as the leadership wished.

In the meantime, the provisional government careened from crisis to crisis. The ministers found actual governing much harder than giving speeches from the floor of the Duma. The government's power began to drain away to the soviet, which represented the mass of citizens and workers in Petrograd.

Soon the country was on the brink of chaos. Dozens,

even hundreds, of murders, lynchings, and robberies took place everyday in Petrograd and other cities.

Meanwhile, the war ground on. The provisional government could not bring itself to pull Russia out. Britain, France, and other allies had promised aid if the provisional government continued the war effort, but it never arrived. The situation was desperate. Withdrawing from the war risked attack from former allies and the end to Russian dreams of Balkan expansion. Continuing probably meant the end of the provisional government.

Attempts to win support from the soldiers by giving them more power also backfired. Soldiers and sailors now elected committees to look out for them; officers no longer had power. This broke down discipline as more and more troops voted to avoid risking their lives in combat.

Despite these problems, the army launched an attack on the eastern front in July. At first, the Russians steamrolled the demoralized Austrians, but a German counterattack stopped the advance. Soon the Russian army was fleeing in chaos, and deserters were rampaging through the Russian countryside.

After the defeat, renewed strikes and demonstrations shook Petrograd. The Bolsheviks faced a problem. If they refused to join the marches, they risked losing credibility. But if they gambled that this was a new revolution against the provisional government, they could lose their own freedom—maybe their lives—if they were wrong. Historians disagree on whether the

Bolsheviks led the uprising or simply tried to steer something that was bound to happen in a direction favorable to them. Whatever the case, many thought the riots were Lenin's attempt to take power. The provisional government, hoping to cripple the Bolshevik trouble-makers, encouraged that idea. Newspaper articles appeared connecting Lenin to the German money he had been given, and the rumor that Lenin was a German spy swept Petrograd. Overnight the Bolsheviks were transformed into a band of traitors. Lenin, believing his life in danger, disappeared.

On Stalin's advice, Lenin hid with the Alliluyev family. Stalin shaved off Lenin's distinctive mustache and beard, while Sergei Alliluyev donated a workman's coat and cap for a disguise. Lenin escaped the government manhunt on board a crowded train. Most of the other Bolshevik leaders were less fortunate. A few managed to hide, but many of the better-known party members, including Kamenev, were arrested. The government considered Stalin to be so unimportant the police didn't bother to pick him up.

Despite this setback, Lenin did not give up on revolution. Nor did he pretend it would be peaceful. He said, "Now it is possible to take power only by means of armed uprising, which will come not later than September or October."

By September, the Russian people were exhausted and angry. The army's commander in chief entered into a plot to get rid of the provisional government. When it looked like the army might help the general dispose of the government, the government pleaded for the revolutionary parties—including the disgraced Bolsheviks—to aid its resistance. As it turned out, the army plot went nowhere, but the provisional government's invitation to the Bolsheviks restored the party's credibility.

Lenin recognized the time had come for a Marxist takeover. To delay was in his mind "disgraceful," "criminal," a "betrayal of the Revolution." But others disagreed. Kamenev and Grigori Zinoviev, perhaps Lenin's closest collaborator, thought the timing was bad. They leaked Bolshevik intentions to local newspapers in hopes of heading off what to them looked like a disastrous uprising. Lenin, furious, demanded that they be expelled from the party.

The Bolshevik leadership, much to Lenin's frustration, held off on setting a date to seize power. But even with the delay, the provisional government was trapped between fear of a Bolshevik takeover on one side and a return of the czar on the other.

Years after 1917, history books in the Soviet Union claimed that Stalin was second only to Lenin as a leader of the Russian Revolution. However, he actually had a much less critical role than the man who would become his greatest rival and, eventually, his most famous victim.

Leon Trotsky was born Lev Davidovich Bronstein on November 7, 1879. The son of an illiterate Jewish farmer, the young Bronstein spent his childhood in a clay house with earthen floors and a leaky thatched roof.

Bronstein grew into a fashion-conscious young man with a dramatic stack of thick black hair. During his college years he drifted into revolutionary politics. Impulsive, passionate, and remarkably self-centered, he first dismissed Marxism as dehumanizing and then, not long after, declared himself an enthusiastic Marxist. No sooner had he done so than, in a characteristic burst of energy, he began to write pamphlets, organize a Marxist

Leon Trotsky. (Courtesy of the Granger Collection.)

workers group, and alienate comrades with his arrogance. In 1897, he began the familiar revolutionary path—arrest, prison, studying in his cell, and his first term of Siberian exile.

In Siberia he cranked out leaflets and articles for Siberian Social Democratic groups. He also wrote on art and the many other topics that interested his wide-ranging intellect. When he read Lenin's *What Is To Be Done?* while in exile, he sensed great things were happening. He escaped and headed west on a fake passport that gave his name as Trotsky. Bold as always, he begged and borrowed his way across Europe until he ended up at Lenin's London apartment in the middle of the night. He and Lenin immediately stepped inside to discuss ideas.

Though he initially admired Lenin, Trotsky refused to take sides in the Bolshevik-Menshevik split, although he tended to favor the Menshevik position on many issues. Trotsky's first fame came during the 1905 revolution, when the twenty-six year-old briefly led the Petrograd Soviet. In the ensuing crackdown, he was sentenced to life in Siberia. En route he escaped—yet another adventure, as he took off aboard a reindeer-sleigh across the tundra—and eventually settled in Vienna. Unlike many Social Democrats, he rarely experienced poverty. He made a living writing for a number of European newspapers and his father, now well-to-do, sometimes sent him cash.

With revolution on the horizon, Trotsky joined the

Bolsheviks in the summer of 1917. His leadership and brilliant public speaking quickly vaulted him to the highest ranks in the party. The quick rise caused resentment among Bolshevik veterans, Stalin included. Trotsky's personality only added to the problem. His self-centeredness and arrogance had only increased over the years. He was brilliant and charismatic, but lacked charm. In short, he had many admirers and few friends. Stalin nursed a personal grudge against him. Ten years before, during the controversy over expropriations, Trotsky had loudly opposed the robberies. In doing so, he had unwittingly crossed Stalin—who never forgot an insult.

As the revolution gained momentum, Trotsky eclipsed everyone but Lenin. As president of the Petrograd Soviet, Trotsky had a high profile. He thrived in the spotlight. On October 22, he stood before a huge meeting and convinced the audience to take an oath of loyalty to the soviet and the revolution. A day later, he showed up at a Petrograd fortress manned by soldiers said to support the provisional government. By the time Trotsky left, the soldiers had taken the same oath. He helped plan the details of the Bolshevik takeover and then spent the eve of the revolution sparring with the Menshevik leaders before a large crowd. Stalin was incapable of competing in such a public arena.

On the morning of October 24, the provisional government finally moved against the Bolsheviks. Policemen smashed their printing press and cut the telephone lines to the Smolny Institute, a onetime girls high school that the Bolsheviks, the Petrograd Soviet, and other aligned groups used as their headquarters.

In retaliation, Stalin and Trotsky organized supporters and gathered and analyzed the information coming in from across the city. Bolshevik activists, along with allied workers, soldiers, and sailors, took over Petrograd's government buildings, communications centers (telegraphs, post offices), railroads, banks, bridges, and the main squares and roads. No shots were fired. Employees and soldiers not loyal to the Bolsheviks were simply sent home. The city's businesses opened as usual the next day. Lenin compared the operation to picking up a feather.

The October Revolution, the Bolshevik seizure of power, was virtually over by morning, with the exception of one important detail. Most of the provisional government's ministers—the Russian nation's legitimate authority—remained holed up in the czar's former Winter Palace. Lenin, nonetheless, gave a short victory speech. "I was seated above and behind the lectern," one Bolshevik remembered, "Lenin is at the lectern. . . . For some reason I remember that Lenin, while addressing the audience, stood with one foot slightly raised as was his style when delivering a speech. The sole of his shoe was visible, and I noticed a hole in it."

This 1935 painting glorifying Lenin's role during the October Revolution is considered part of the socialist realism school, which sought to promote the goals of socialism and communism through technically realistic portrayals. (Courtesy of Art Resource.)

Armed Bolshevik supporters, called the Red Guards, sneaked inside the Winter Palace several times, only to flee when confronted by pro-government soldiers. Eventually, as hope of relief faded, the troops loyal to the provincial government drifted away, until all that remained were teenaged students from a military school and female soldiers of the dramatically named Women's Death Battalion. They barely resisted when the Red Guards entered. Soon the ministers were under arrest.

When the Bolsheviks convened a congress to ratify their illegal takeover, it immediately disintegrated into arguments between the Mensheviks and Bolsheviks. The Mensheviks condemned the Bolshevik coup and marched out of the meeting hall as Trotsky cried, "You are pitiful, isolated individuals. You are bankrupts; your role is played out. Go where you belong from now on: into the rubbish-can of history!"

Lenin immediately issued three decrees that carried through on previous Bolshevik promises. The first called for a cease-fire at the front. The second confiscated land from landlords and the Russian state and church, to be turned over to the peasants. The third announced the formation of a new government, with Lenin in charge. This government, the Bolsheviks said, would only serve until a democratically elected Constituent Assembly came together. Lenin had no intention of honoring this promise; he hoped to buy the time the Bolsheviks needed to strengthen their hold on power. Trotsky headed foreign policy. Stalin took charge of an entirely new department, Nationality Affairs, dealing with the non-Russian peoples of the old empire. As a Georgian and a published theorist on the subject, he seemed a natural choice for the job.

Stalin kept such a low profile during these dramatic times that one day he would have to rewrite history to convince the world otherwise. Though capable as an editor and organizer, he lacked the charismatic gifts of Lenin or Trotsky. He was later dismissed as unimportant to the cause, but that was not true either. During the October Revolution, Stalin performed practical tasks, the type that any political movement, regardless of its beliefs, needs in order to get things done. That Lenin afterward chose Stalin for a leadership role proves he carried out his work well.

Following the October Revolution, everyone praised the thinkers and forgot the practicals. Sukhanov, the Menshevik eyewitness to the Revolution, remembered that "[Stalin] gave me the impression—and not me alone—of a gray blur sometimes emitting a dim and inconsequential light. There is really nothing more to be said about him." In 1920, the Bolshevik government published a photomontage of its revolutionary heroes. Over seventy faces appeared. Stalin was not one of them. It was a slight he would never forget and, as was often the case with him, could not forgive.

Four

CIVIL WAR

Few inside or outside of Russia thought the Bolsheviks would be able to hold on to power for long. Even committed Marxists, such as the writer Maxim Gorky, thought Lenin had taken control prematurely. The fact that the Bolsheviks had problems just getting into their offices because the provisional government's bureaucrats refused to turn over keys was seen as a bad omen.

Stalin's Department of Nationality Affairs had no money and was not a high priority. He relied on a barebones staff that included Nadezhda "Nadya" Alliluyeva, the Alliluyev family's high-spirited teenaged daughter, and her brother Fyodor.

Despite the obstacles, Stalin got down to the urgent work facing his department. The instability that followed the czar's overthrow had encouraged independence movements among many ethnic groups. Lenin had yet to develop a policy on the nationalities beyond the declaration that the czar's repression had ended, but he desperately wanted them to remain a part of the new Soviet state. His hopes of keeping different nationalities joined to Russia rested on local Social Democrats in those regions seizing power and electing to become a part of a union of Socialist nations. In that way he could avoid using force.

Finland offered Lenin and Stalin a chance to test the Bolshevik policy. In mid-November, Stalin told a meeting of the country's Social Democrats that Lenin's government intended to grant Finland independence (Finland had been annexed by Russia in 1809). Lenin believed that once Finland was independent, the Finnish Social Democrats would start a revolution and take power, and Finland would join a union of Socialist nations controlled by Russia. But the Finnish Social Democrats refused to seize power, and an anti-Bolshevik government took office. It was the first of many errors in judgment that Lenin and Stalin would make about revolutionary feeling in other countries.

Russia was still officially at war with Germany. Lenin wanted to negotiate a peace treaty, even though Germany was certain to exact a heavy price. Trotsky, who was head of foreign affairs, opposed the idea. He argued that if Russia simply stopped fighting and Germany saw it was no longer a threat, Germany would shift its armies to the western front. The U.S. had entered the war on the Allied side, and Germany would need all its troops in France and Belgium to stop the coming attack.

Trotsky also thought there would soon be a Marxist uprising in Germany, just as there had been in Russia. After it seized power, this new workers' government would become Russia's ally. To negotiate a peace treaty, Trotsky argued, would undercut the German Marxists.

Stalin was unimpressed with Trotsky's reasoning: "Comrade Trotsky's position is not a position at all. There's no revolutionary movement in the West." Stalin's practical skepticism proved to be accurate. In mid-February, the Germans, unimpressed by Trotsky's scheme, renewed their march into Russian territory. The Bolshevik government fled from Petrograd to Moscow to escape the threat. Lenin insisted the government reopen negotiations with Germany and quickly agree on a treaty. As usual, Lenin did not sugarcoat what he meant. "If you don't sign [the treaty], then you will be signing the death sentence of the Soviet government . . . of that, I haven't the slightest shadow of a doubt."

Lenin argued that the biggest threat to a Marxist revolution in other parts of Europe would be if Germany destroyed the Bolshevik government in Russia. The agreement that was eventually signed, the Treaty of Brest-Litovsk, was harsh. Russia gave up territory that included 62 million people, three-fourths of the country's iron and coal mines, a third of its agricultural land, and a third of its factories. The cost was enormous, but Lenin had his breathing space.

Lenin was right; the Soviet government desperately needed peace. Russia's internal problems, bad under Nicholas and the provisional government, had spun further out of control since the October Revolution. Basic law and order had broken down. Looting, property seizures, lynch mobs, and deadly rampages by soldiers raged throughout the vast country.

Political disorder also threatened the new government. In the Bolsheviks' minds, a host of political and class enemies, both real and imagined, might at any minute start a counterrevolution against them. In response, the Bolsheviks created a secret police force known as the Cheka, both to fight their enemies and to terrify the rest of the country into accepting Bolshevik rule. Members of the upper classes, opponents in the bureaucracy, aristocrats, military officers, and clergymen were shot or thrown into prison by the thousands.

Bolshevik policies in the countryside added to the ongoing violence. Marx's writings had said relatively little about peasants. The Bolsheviks, however, headed a country with an enormous peasant population. Lenin had to adapt Marxist thinking to include them. He did this by replicating, in theory, the class conflict that existed between workers and capitalists. The poorest peasants played the role of workers, and the more successful peasants and small landowners, called *kulaks*, took the role of capitalists. In reality, most kulaks were only slightly better off than their neighbors. But the Bolsheviks needed an enemy for their class war, and the kulaks were filled the role.

Unrest on the farms contributed to another crisis: hunger in the cities. "Petrograd is in an unprecedentedly catastrophic condition," the government declared. "There is no bread. The population is given the remaining potato flour and crusts. The Red capital is on the verge of perishing from famine." Even in areas with surplus food, peasants once again refused to sell to the government. The food that wasn't turned into liquor or livestock feed went into the thriving black market.

Lenin responded to food hoarding with extreme measures. Under a policy he dubbed War Communism, armed groups of workers and soldiers were sent into the countryside to confiscate surplus grain and other food. In places out of the Bolsheviks' reach, the government encouraged poor peasants to raid the kulaks by allowing them to keep a share of whatever they found. But the peasants' life continued to be miserable, and many blamed the Bolsheviks. "[You say] the land belongs to us, but the bread belongs to you," one man complained. "The water belongs to us, but the fish to you; the forests are ours, but the timber is yours."

By the end of May, the cities were desperate for food. Bolshevik leaders went to the country to see the situation themselves. Stalin, accompanied by the Alliluyev siblings, took a hair-raising train journey to Tsaritsyn,

Stalin on the Tsaritsyn front in 1918. (Courtesy of Getty Images.)

a transportation center and the key to one of southern Russia's major agricultural areas. He found the city in chaos and, with the ruthlessness that would become his signature, ordered executions for anyone he suspected, even on the skimpiest of evidence, of black market activity or collaboration with counterrevolutionaries.

Throughout the spring, a number of anti-Bolshevik armies had taken shape outside the zone the government controlled in central Russia. Nicknamed the Whites, as opposed to the Bolshevik Reds, these often ragged forces drew officers from the czar's old army and other

Tzaritsyn would be renamed Stalingrad in 1925. In 1961, the city's name was changed to Volgograd, in reference to its position on the Volga River.

groups opposed to Red rule. Soon France and Britain, infuriated at Lenin's separate peace, were giving the Whites funds, supplies, and small numbers of support troops. Lenin ordered Trotsky, the new commissar of war, to organize and lead the Red Army. Trotsky leapt into the job with his usual energy, roaring from front to front in his armored train and overseeing operations all over the country. The position would win him even more glory.

When White forces threatened Tsaritsyn in the summer, Stalin thought he was best suited to take charge. Like many Bolsheviks, he was suspicious of the military specialists and officers Trotsky had recruited from the czar's army to help the Red cause. Rightly or wrongly, Stalin blamed them for Tsaritsyn's precarious situation. "For the good of the cause I must have military powers," he wrote to Lenin. When he did not receive a reply, he took matters into his own hands and shot some of the military men he thought were sabotaging the cause and locked up the rest on a river barge. According to some accounts, he then sank the barge.

Throughout the summer, Stalin ignored orders from the government in general and Trotsky in particular. When Trotsky's appointed commander arrived on the Tsaritsyn front, Stalin removed him without permission. Trotsky, exasperated, telegraphed Lenin: "I categorically insist that Stalin be recalled." Stalin left for Moscow soon after, his ruthlessness at Tsaritsyn adding to his reputation as a strong, decisive leader. When the Bolshevik Party established an elite political bureau,

A Russian Civil War White Army propaganda poster depicting Trotsky as a Jewish devil. (Library of Congress)

called the Politburo, to decide vital issues, Stalin was chosen as one of its five members.

Over the new year, Stalin and Trotsky had more conflicts. Trotsky was still the more colorful and better-known leader, but Stalin was proving to be the superior politician.

By 1920, the civil war was winding down toward a Red victory. But a new military situation had developed. Poland, which had been under Russian control since the eighteenth century, had been granted independence after World War I. Almost immediately, the new nation invaded the Ukraine and parts of western Russia to reclaim areas it considered Polish. The Red Army counterattacked and rolled the Poles back. At that point, the national question reared its head once again. Should the Red Army let newly independent Poland go, or push on into Polish territory to "convince" them to remain linked to Russia? The collapse of Germany and the end of World War I complicated the question. Maybe this was the time to send the Red Army into the West to inspire Social Democrats in Germany and elsewhere, Trotsky and the internationalists said. Why settle for Poland when all of Europe might be on the brink of Socialist revolution?

It was an old dream, and this time even the usually levelheaded Lenin was sucked in. But to Stalin, Poland looked like a bad place to start inciting revolutions. Lenin's prowar faction counted on the Polish working class rising up and aiding the Soviet invaders. Stalin argued that the workers would support the Polish government out of patriotism. The average Pole hated Russia much more than it did its own government. Lenin had often trusted Stalin's insights on the nationalities, but this time he ignored the advice. As head of the world's only Marxist state, he believed the Bolsheviks had a duty to help the working class elsewhere.

The crusade to spread revolution quickly turned into a disaster. Poland's working class, as Stalin predicted, resisted the hated Russians. The Red Army, already exhausted by the civil war, became bogged down in a two-week battle outside Warsaw. Stalin's habit of refusing to listen to orders also played a part. When the military leadership directed him to send part of his forces north, he held back the requested men for an operation of his own. During the finger-pointing that followed the invasion, Stalin was accused of insubordination, incompetence, and putting his career before the good of the cause. Nothing came of the charges, and Stalin put on a stoic face. But it seems likely Stalin felt insulted, all the more so because Trotsky backed up many of the accusations. Even Lenin, who Stalin considered to be most responsible for the disaster, criticized him.

Stalin's moment of disgrace passed quickly. In fact, Lenin continued to take an interest in him. He helped Stalin find an apartment in Moscow—a difficult task at the time—and made sure he got proper care when he came down with appendicitis.

After the fiasco in Poland, the Bolsheviks shelved the dream of European revolution and focused on problems within Russia. The country had endured years of war, Red Terror, civil war, and innumerable acts of violence, ranging from anti-Semitic pogroms, or massacres, to ethnic cleansing to the murder of the czar and his family.

These horrors were only the beginning. Thousands continued to die from cold and disease. Then a severe drought struck some of Russia's agricultural regions in early 1921 and continued through a blazing summer. The Soviet government had seized the grain the peasants kept in reserve, and now nothing remained. The famine's death toll was over five million.

Industry and finance were wrecked. Many of the

experts, considered class enemies by the Bolsheviks, had left Russia, and it was still difficult to get raw materials to the factories. The Soviet government hoped to sell raw materials to the West, but few countries were willing to do business with them.

A clear signal that change was needed came in March 1921. The Kronstadt naval base, once a stronghold of pro-Bolshevik feeling, revolted. This came at a time when peasants' uprisings were shaking rural areas. Though the Kronstadt rebellion was put down, Lenin cancelled the strategy of War Communism and instituted in its place the New Economic Policy, or NEP.

The NEP called for a mixed economy, combining aspects of socialism and capitalism. On the Socialist side, the Soviet government kept its ownership of Russia's largest industries and the transportation system, and maintained overall control of the economy. But it encouraged a limited form of capitalism by allowing private ownership of some trade, as well as medium-sized industries and businesses. In addition, the government invited Western countries to invest in Russian business. Because the NEP encouraged a measure of Western-style market economics guided somewhat by supply and demand, it offended some Bolsheviks. But Lenin was willing to bend his principles when necessary to put Russia back on its feet.

Lenin simultaneously addressed problems within the Communist Party, the official name adopted by the Bolsheviks and the government. Day-to-day operations

ИЗ РОССИИ
НЭПОВСКОЙ
БУДЕТ РОССИЯ
СОЦИАЛИСТИЧЕСКАЯ
(ЛЕНИН)

Soviet propaganda art played an essential role in the popular appeal of the Revolution. In this poster, Lenin is quoted as saying, "From NEP Russia will come Socialist Russia." (Library of Congress)

were a constant frustration. Corruption, inefficiency, and red tape slowed government business to a crawl;

there were too few competent civil servants. Solving problems required a major housecleaning. Lenin needed a ruthless manager able to make changes. Stalin was the man for the job.

Few people envied Stalin's new assignment. It was unglamorous and time-consuming and involved the grinding work of reorganizing at all levels. But Stalin was a workhorse, with little patience for the debate and innumerable meetings that were a part of Bolshevik culture. His tantrums soon became legendary, as did his need to take revenge for even small transgressions. This trait was even given a name—Stalin's Theory of Sweet Revenge. He once admitted to Kamenev, "The greatest delight is to mark one's enemy, prepare everything, avenge oneself thoroughly, and then go to sleep."

Despite Stalin's personal shortcomings, he worked harder than anyone else. He was appointed general secretary of the Communist Party on April 3, 1922, which put him in charge of day-to-day operations. Although the Politburo made the decisions, it was the general secretary that provided the resources and information needed to carry out Politburo orders. Stalin's power now reached into every corner of society. The secretary made assignments, awarded promotions, hired and fired workers, allotted resources, oversaw party organizations, issued orders, and coordinated a dizzying number of government and Communist Party programs. Stalin promoted his people to key jobs, who then hired and promoted their people, who in turn became

Stalin's people. Other Soviet leaders acquired a similar following, but it was usually limited to their own areas. No one had Stalin's influence across the nation and up and down the ranks of the party.

Two weeks after Stalin's appointment, Lenin suffered a stroke that left him temporarily paralyzed and almost unable to speak. He was taken to the country to recover. Stalin, being general secretary, had the job of overseeing his care. Lenin was the Communist Party's most valuable resource. Throughout the summer, Stalin visited Lenin to report on various matters. Back in Moscow, Stalin settled into his work as general secretary. Usually cautious, he now began to act with more self-confidence, rudeness, and arrogance. Cronies rose to good positions, those who crossed him were demoted or reassigned.

Stalin's power was growing, but problems in the Nationality Affairs department threatened it. Ethnic violence had broken out in his native Caucasus region. Most ominously, Georgia had declared independence. Lenin had ordered an invasion, but he first wanted to try to tempt the Georgians into the new union—eventually to be called the Union of Soviet Socialist Republics (USSR)—with compromises appealing to their national ambitions.

Stalin, never a patient man, went along with Lenin's strategy for a while, but by 1922, he was frustrated with the policy of persuasion and ordered his associates in Tiflis to apply pressure. When he heard news of the brutal tactics Stalin had ordered, Lenin publicly criticized

Stalin. Lenin even began to gather his own information on Georgia instead of relying on the office of the general secretary for intelligence.

The tension continued when Lenin returned to work in the fall. Looking around, he saw more reasons to doubt Stalin. Government inefficiency and red tape seemed worse than before. Even Lenin's orders sometimes got lost in the shuffle. But before he could correct the situation, Lenin suffered another stroke on December 12, 1922. Even though he recovered slightly, Lenin's health was obviously fading. The Soviet leadership had to consider a question: who could replace Lenin?

Lenin was under doctor's orders to avoid the stress of politics. On December 21, however, he asked his wife, Nadezhda Krupskaya, to take dictation on an admiring

Stalin visits with an ailing Lenin in 1922. (Courtesy of Getty Images.)

letter to Trotsky. Stalin was enraged when he learned of the letter. Via telephone he berated Krupskaya and accused of her of endangering Lenin's health. The shaken Krupskaya kept the conversation from Lenin, at first. But Stalin had committed an error.

Lenin was in the final phase of his life. Increasingly ill, and working to relearn how to talk and write, he nevertheless began to organize an attack on Stalin, who learned some of the details from one of Lenin's secretaries. There was little he could do but wait for the attack and hope Lenin died before it could be launched.

In early March, Trotsky received copies of notes Lenin had written in December that indicated Lenin had turned against Stalin. Lenin sent Stalin a personal letter:

> Respected Comrade Stalin,
>
> You had the rudeness to call my wife to the telephone to abuse her. Although she expressed her willingness to forget what was said, the fact became known, through her, to Zinoviev and Kamenev.
>
> I do not wish to forget so easily what was done against me, and there is no need to point out that what is done against my wife I consider to be against me also. Therefore I ask you to consider whether you agree to take back what you said and apologize, or whether you prefer to break relations between us.
>
> With respect,
> Lenin

Stalin now faced the greatest threat of his political life. He admitted screaming at Krupskaya but claimed the incident came out of his duty to protect Lenin. In conclusion, he said, "Yet if you consider that the maintenance of 'relations' requires me to 'retract' the above-mentioned words, I can retract them, while nevertheless refusing to understand what the problem is here, what my 'guilt' consists of and what in particular is being demanded of me."

It is unclear whether or not Lenin ever read Stalin's halfhearted words, but it is likely Lenin still intended to come out against Stalin at the party congress scheduled for March. As a preview, Lenin wrote an attack on Stalin's administrative abilities that was so scathing the leadership hesitated to publish it. Stalin, not surprisingly, voted against publication; but Trotsky and Kamenev, in rare agreement, thought any article by Lenin had to be released. Its appearance in *Pravda* hurt Stalin politically and personally. He had idolized Lenin for twenty years, had done thankless and dangerous work on his orders, had enjoyed his trust and come to see himself as the great man's natural replacement. And now Lenin was determined to destroy him.

Fate intervened on March 10, 1923. Another severe stroke took away Lenin's power to speak and write. He never recovered. But Stalin had little time to feel relieved. The struggle for power had begun.

Five
STALIN'S RISE TO POWER

The struggle for of the Communist Party and the USSR began before Lenin was dead. Stalin started off at a definite disadvantage. The party congress took place that spring during the Georgia crisis. Lenin had intended to unseat Stalin during the congress, and he had urged Trotsky to speak on his behalf in the Georgian affair. Trotsky was generally assumed to be Lenin's preferred successor, and this presented him an opportunity to take down Stalin.

When the congress opened, Trotsky received the most enthusiastic applause, always a sign of party approval. It felt like Trotsky's coronation, but he then, inexplicably, passed up the opportunity to attack Stalin. When it was his turn, the general secretary gave a report that claimed he was following party policy and condemned the Georgian leadership for putting nationalism above the revolution.

Trotsky had allowed Stalin to slip off the hook with only a promise to behave better in the future, although Lenin had specifically warned that Stalin would use just that trick to avoid censure. Why Trotsky backed off at this critical moment remains a mystery. It might have been because he was disliked by many veteran Bolsheviks, or he sensed that trying to unseat Stalin would look like an attempt to take power before Lenin had died. Whatever his reasons, it was a decision he would eventually pay for with his life.

Emboldened, Stalin began to act as he had before Lenin's illness. He formed a working partnership with two other leaders. Kamenev was the head of Moscow's Communist Party. Although he did not hate Trotsky the way Stalin did, Kamenev thought he was an unsuitable replacement for Lenin. Kamenev worked in tandem with Grigori Zinoviev, the party's boss in Petrograd. Many considered Zinoviev's chances of succeeding Lenin second only to Trotsky's. His time as a Bolshevik dated back to 1903, and for a long time he had been Lenin's closest disciple. However, he lacked respect inside the party. Many remembered his misstep before the October Revolution, when he and Kamenev had leaked the Bolshevik intentions to a local newspaper. Zinoviev despised Trotsky, who had relieved him of a military command during the Civil War.

Dislike for Trotsky, either political, personal, or both, united Zinoviev and Kamenev with Stalin. At first they considered Stalin the junior partner. This did not seem to bother the general secretary, who often spoke in favor of group leadership. In truth, neither side of the partnership trusted the other.

Trotsky, meanwhile, maintained a low profile. While his rivals plotted his downfall, he kept busy writing speeches on nonpolitical topics that ranged from psychology to vodka to family life. It was only when Stalin and Zinoviev moved to limit his power in the Red Army that Trotsky decided to fight. He accused Stalin of using his position to smother dissenting views. Many party leaders agreed with Trotsky's charge, but when it came time for a showdown, he pled illness and retreated. In his absence, Stalin engineered an overwhelming vote against Trotsky.

Lenin died on January 21, 1924. Thousands gathered in Moscow's Red Square to mourn and to watch for signs of who might be the new leader. Stalin, Zinoviev, and Kamenev served as pallbearers, and Stalin, as general secretary, organized the funeral. To the amazement of party members then and historians ever after, Trotsky failed to attend. He had been on medical leave in the south when he heard the news. Later he claimed the Politburo switched the funeral's dates on him; but he also admitted, "I knew only one urgent desire—and that was to be left alone."

Lenin's embalmed body was installed in a new

Lenin's coffin is carried from Paveletsky Station to the Dom Soyouson (Larch Temple) in Moscow. His pallbearers included Kalinin, Bukharin, Tomsky, Kamenev, Stalin, and Zinoviev. (Courtesy of Getty Images.)

mausoleum for public display. This was against Lenin's expressed wishes. He had hated the glorification of leaders because it smacked too much of czarism. But the mausoleum was the start of a campaign to turn Lenin into a sort of Communist demigod. Stalin gave a eulogy filled with blatantly religious language. Clearly, the former seminary student understood religion's power.

Lenin had dictated a so-called testament that suggested changes in the party's political structure. But it was his comments on each of the party leaders that overshadowed everything else. Stalin feared the reaction to what had been written about him. He, Zinoviev, and Kamenev saw to it that the testament was not read to the entire congress, but instead to separate groups of representatives. No discussion was allowed, nor could they refer to it in public.

Kamenev read Lenin's testament to the Central Committee on May 21. In the text, Lenin complimented Trotsky and Stalin as the outstanding members of the leadership but worried that their poor relationship could split the Party. Furthermore, Lenin wondered if Stalin could be trusted to use his great power with "sufficient caution," and added a scathing note on the vices of the general secretary:

> Stalin is too rude and this defect, although quite tolerable . . . in dealings among us Communists, becomes intolerable in a general secretary. That is why I suggest that the comrades think about a way of transferring Stalin from that post and appointing another man in his stead who in all other respects differs from Comrade Stalin in having only one advantage, namely, that of being more tolerant, more loyal, more polite and more considerate to comrades, less capricious, etc. This circumstance may appear to be a mere trifle. But I think that from the standpoint of safeguards against a split [in the party] and from the standpoint of what I wrote . . . about the relationship between Stalin and Trotsky it is not a mere trifle, or it is a trifle which can assume decisive importance.

"Painful embarrassment paralyzed the whole gathering," one of Stalin's assistants wrote. "Despite his self-control and forced calm, one could clearly read in his face the fact that his fate was being decided."

Clearly, Lenin had meant to replace Stalin. Now, in the current mournful atmosphere, it seemed unthinkable that his dying wish would be ignored. Zinoviev and Kamenev, however, knew the loss of their partner would be a victory for the hated Trotsky. They convinced the Central Committee to keep Stalin by pointing out how his behavior had been exemplary since Lenin's death. Stalin survived, and when the dust settled he turned to improving his image within the party.

Leading the USSR required more than a job title. A reputation as an intellectual was vital. Stalin published *The Foundations of Leninism*, which boiled down Lenin's massive volume of writings to an easily understood set of rules. The more accomplished writers in the party looked down on a book written for less sophisticated readers, but *The Foundations of Leninism* proved Stalin had the better political instincts. Of the many books on Lenin's ideas that appeared after his death, Stalin's was the most popular. The reason was simple. By the mid-1920s, the Communist Party had tens of thousands of new members, many of them poorly educated. While Trotsky's complex theories and literary language meant little to them, Stalin straightforward words answered many of their questions about the new government and its ideology.

The struggle for power began to turn decisively against Trotsky. Every harsh word Trotsky had ever exchanged with Lenin found its way into print. That he only joined the Bolsheviks in 1917 was brought up again and again. While he could truthfully say, "I came to Lenin fighting, but I came to him fully," he had always remained an outsider. The Stalin-Zinoviev-Kamenev group used every resource to demonize him. Trotsky was transformed into Lenin's fallen angel, the Satan of the Bolshevik Revolution.

Trotsky, ill and discouraged by his lack of support, resigned as war commissar. Now, with his power base lost and his followers forced out of their jobs, he served on the Politburo without allies or influence.

With Trotsky shunted aside, the bond uniting Stalin with Zinoviev and Kamenev began to show strain. The general secretary began to replace *their* supporters in the party. The New Economic Policy became one of the primary battlefields.

The Soviet economy had shown modest recovery under the NEP. Some foreign trade had resumed, and goods made their way around the USSR again, led by a new class of entrepreneurs nicknamed *nepmen*. In the countryside the kulaks found it easier to turn a profit. Though nepmen and kulaks played an important part in the new economy, many in the Communist Party considered them, at best, a necessary evil, and, at worst, class enemies. But the pro-NEP faction focused on the fact that the policy provided stability. To them the NEP could be a useful tool for slowly rebuilding the country's economic strength before the transition to socialism.

Stalin knew Zinoviev and Kamenev opposed keeping the NEP. He turned to pro-NEP party members as new allies in the coming showdown with his former allies. This dovetailed with a new direction in his thinking. Stalin had recently suggested that the Soviet Union should, if necessary, forget about revolutions in other countries and build socialism in the USSR. This idea went against a strongly held belief that the Soviet Union could not survive without Marxist allies in the world. It also ignored the old revolutionary hope of spreading

This 1926 satire of the upper class by Bolshevik artist Vladimir Kozlinsky is entitled "Sympathy." Its subtitle reads, "Nepmenshi [NEP women]: Girl! Don't touch the dog, please! It might catch something from you."

Marxism to Europe and beyond, hopes that went back to the earliest days of the Bolshevik movement and were held not only by Trotsky.

Stalin again proved himself to be the more ruthless politician. Having already demonized Trotsky, he used the same tactics against his old partners. The pair inevitably heard the old stories about how they tried to sabotage the October Revolution by going to the newspapers. They were also accused of personal ambition at a time when unity was essential, a hypocritical statement to say the least. But Zinoviev and Kamenev couldn't keep up with the attacks.

The upswing in Stalin's career paralleled changes in his personal life. He was now a respected family man. During the civil war he had married Nadya Alliluyeva, his teenaged secretary at Nationality Affairs.

By all accounts the couple began their marriage deeply in love. But Stalin seems to have expected a traditional Georgian marriage—a dominant husband and a submissive homemaker wife. Nadya was a Bolshevik idealist, willing to head off to the south during the civil war, and trusted enough to serve as one of Lenin's secretaries. Communist Party culture idealized the working class—living modestly, roughing it when necessary—and Nadya took that to heart. In 1921, she walked to the hospital to give birth to her son, Vasily. Later in the decade, she insisted on taking public transportation to her classes at an industrial college, despite the fact that her husband was the most powerful man in the

Stalin and Nadya on a picnic with friends in the 1920s. (Novosti Photo Library, London)

USSR. Their modest lifestyle reflected well on Stalin. While Kamenev used a Rolls Royce, for example, Stalin rode in an old Russian car. Many leading Bolsheviks entertained a steady stream of mistresses. Stalin, in the 1920s anyway, had little interest in women, including, as time went on, his wife.

Nadya's energy and humor made her an excellent politician's wife. When Stalin, like all the Bolshevik elite, acquired a country house, Nadya entertained family and party members alike, and helped paper over some of her husband's gruff moments. But all was not well at the Stalin home. The couple had horrible fights and long periods when they refused to speak. Stalin resented that Nadya wanted her own career. For her part Nadya was strong willed and bad tempered. "She was very beautiful at times," an observer said, "and very ugly at others—it depended on her mood." Nadya quite likely suffered from psychological or emotional problems, including severe depression.

The battle for power resumed. In April 1926, Zinoviev and Kamenev asked their old enemy for help. "It will be enough for you and Zinoviev to appear on the platform in order to reconquer the whole party," Kamenev exclaimed to Trotsky, who had his doubts. But his health had improved, and he agreed to make a determined effort to wrest power from the general secretary.

The trio and their followers, calling themselves the United Opposition, spoke out against government policy and leadership. Lenin's widow, Krupskaya, supported them, as did a number of second-tier officials. Stalin, in an effort to panic Zinoviev into breaking with his allies, arranged his expulsion from the Politburo. His place and those of five secondary members were taken by Stalin's followers. The United Opposition went down quickly. Stalin, not satisfied with mere victory, demanded they take back everything they had said. Trotsky refused and, at a wild Politburo meeting, predicted the party's destruction. Pointing to Stalin, he cried, "The first [General] Secretary poses his candidature to the post of the gravedigger of the Revolution." Stalin, barely able to contain himself, stormed out of the room.

Trotsky launched his last attack in 1927. Tensions in the countryside and trouble abroad had shaken up the party. The remains of the old opposition put the blame on Stalin and his allies. Having no outlet to reach the public, they returned to old revolutionary tactics— secret speeches, underground publications. But Stalin sent the secret police to destroy their printing press and break up their demonstrations.

Stalin had Trotsky, Zinoviev, Kamenev, and hundreds of their supporters, including many veteran Bolsheviks, thrown out of the party. In time, and after a lot of humiliation, Zinoviev and Kamenev returned, but on January 17, 1928, secret police agents put Trotsky on a train to Alma Ata, a Central Asian city near the Chinese border. A year later he was exiled forever from the USSR.

Stalin was not yet a total dictator, but he controlled enough of the Politburo and Central Committee to assume power. His ambitions, however, went beyond political leadership. He wanted to prove that he was worthy of the new government slogan, "Stalin is the Lenin of today!" He took any comment critical of the government—or of Marxism itself—as criticism of him personally. He distrusted anyone who questioned his ideas, regardless of their motives. In his mind they became more than political opponents. They were enemies of the Soviet Union.

Once during a vacation, he gestured to his black boots and noted how "convenient" they were. "That way," he said, "you can give certain comrades a kick in their ugly mugs that'll knock their teeth out." The kick in the teeth had become his preferred method of getting things done.

Six

THE SECOND REVOLUTION

With Zinoviev and Kamenev's defeat, the New Economic Policy seemed to be saved. Stalin's pro-NEP allies looked forward to using the market system to gradually improve the Soviet economy. Their hope was that over a generation or two, the USSR could complete the transition to full socialism. It was with complete astonishment, then, that those allies watched as Stalin turned against the NEP mere weeks after using it as a weapon against his rivals.

Stalin's support for the NEP had only been tactical. Now he proposed taking the country in a new direction. The Soviet Union would build socialism by itself. But instead of using the semi-capitalist NEP, he intended to restructure the entire economy, and Soviet society, with

Marxist principles. He called the new direction Socialism in One Country and said it was a second revolution. He also quickly showed that he meant to use violence, if necessary, to impose this second revolution on millions of Soviet citizens.

By late 1927, the peasants were again withholding grain and causing food shortages in the cities. Early in 1928, Stalin and a group of assistants headed into the countryside to gather grain. Communist Party officials in agricultural areas were ordered to do the same—at all costs. Armed squads entered villages and collected food at gunpoint. Kulaks, or people said to be kulaks, were arrested. When Stalin and the grain got back to Moscow, *Pravda* sang his praises, but many in the Soviet leadership did not. Stalin had acted without a vote or even a hint at what he planned to do.

Stalin lashed out at those complaining about the collections, including Nikolai Bukharin, the onetime leader of the pro-NEP faction and Stalin's ally in the battle against Zinoviev and Kamenev. Bukharin was one of the more interesting Bolshevik veterans. A talented writer and intellectual, he had been close to Lenin and was at his bedside when he died. Despite the ugliness of the leadership fight, Bukharin had remained on friendly terms with Zinoviev and Kamenev, while also socializing with Stalin and becoming Nadya's close friend and confidant. But now Bukharin was an obstacle to Stalin's plans.

Stalin wanted to build up Soviet industry quickly.

Nikolai Bukharin in the late 1920s. (Courtesy of Getty Images.)

He knew the USSR remained vulnerable because of the superior industrial and technological development of the West. The gradual transition to socialism that Bukharin hoped to achieve through the NEP would never happen, he argued, because the West would not give them enough time before attacking. "To slacken the pace [of industry] would mean to lag behind; and those who lag behind are beaten," Stalin said in a speech that foreshadowed his brutal plans for the future.

Marxism promised that a government controlled by the working class would decide what products were produced and how they would be distributed. In this command economy, economic decisions were made by the government, as opposed to the capitalist market economy, which is controlled by privately held business and driven by the profit motive of thousands of different companies. Lenin had altered Marxist theory by placing the government in the hands of a small group of leaders, the Communist Party, instead of a more broadly based workers' state that theoretically held power in the name of the working class. Stalin was now determined to use that power to radically modernize the Soviet economy.

Rapid industrialization, however, required vast sums of money to build factories, to buy advanced technology, and to train a workforce. Western countries were unwilling to make loans to a Communist country, however, which meant the Soviet government had to raise the cash through the sale of raw materials. Agricultural products, especially grain, were their most profitable exports. But to increase grain production presented another dilemma: farmers needed machinery, fertilizers, and other technologies, yet the nation could not acquire those technologies unless farmers grew more grain.

Stalin wanted to sell the excess grain peasants had been hoarding to foreign countries to raise capital. Under the NEP, peasant farmers had sold their surplus at government-controlled low prices. Hopes for a price increase had encouraged some to hold back part of their crop. To Stalin this was capitalistic profit taking. He decided it was time to force the peasants into the new, Marxist-Leninist economic system. He made it clear his methods would be harsh. "It is not a matter of caressing the peasant and seeing in this the way to establish correct relations with him," he said, "for you won't go far on caresses."

Bukharin preferred to use a caress. During the NEP years, he had encouraged capitalist-minded peasants to develop their farms without fear of restrictions or the threat of loss. Now he had to take back those promises, but he had not given up on the idea of steady economic growth as a path to socialism. At first Stalin tried to compromise with him. "You and I are the Himalayas," Stalin said. "All the others [in the Party] are nonentities. Let's reach an understanding." To the surprise of everyone, however, Bukharin refused Stalin's offer. Stalin's forces retaliated in the usual way, through a campaign of distortions, lies, and outrageous charges, followed by Bukharin being tossed out of the Politburo.

Bukharin had observed Stalin for a long time and recognized what he was up against. "[Stalin] is an unscrupulous intriguer who subordinates everything to the preservation of his power," he said. "He changes theories depending on whom he wants to get rid of at the moment." However, unlike the fight with Trotsky, this break destroyed one of Stalin's few friendships. For years they had called one another "Stalin" and "Nikolai." Bukharin brought wild animals from his private zoo and gave them as pets to Stalin's children. But none of that mattered now. Bukharin had to go.

In the spring of 1929, the party released the first Five-Year Plan, a blueprint for rapid industrialization. The plan demanded impossible production goals from the

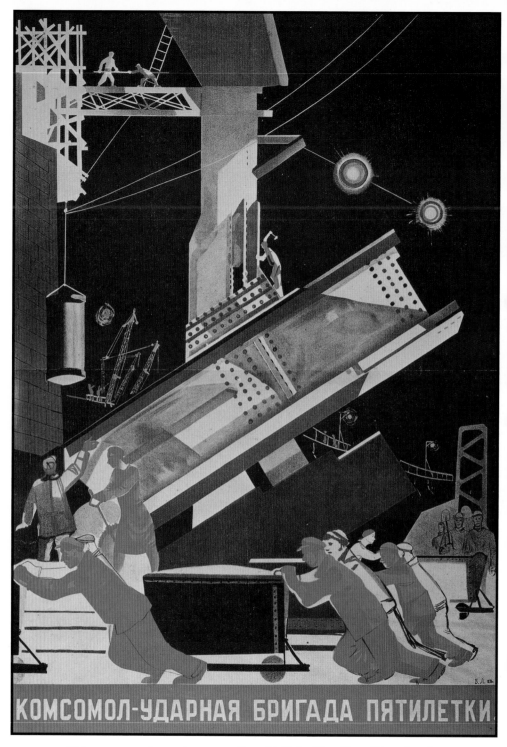

КОМСОМОЛ-УДАРНАЯ БРИГАДА ПЯТИЛЕТКИ

This propaganda poster promoting Stalin's Five-Year Plan for the industrialization of Russia proclaims, "The Young Communist League is the Shock Battalion of the Five-Year Plan." (Courtesy of the Granger Collection.)

country's primitive industries and ordered the creation of entire new ones from scratch. When it came to setting the goals, Stalin did not let his ignorance of economics or industrial matters stop him. Independent scholars and economists tried to reason with him, but to no avail. Instead, he had his yes-men in the Communist Party support the unrealistic plans with dubious reports.

For rapid industrialization to succeed, the peasants had to produce more food. At the end of 1929, Stalin began a radical transformation of agriculture. The first obstacle was the kulaks, which had begun to prosper under NEP. Usually hardworking and enterprising, many had bought plots of land to add to their existing farms and had hired farmhands. Although very few were rich, Stalin needed a class enemy to rally the other farmers around his plan to reorganize agriculture into communal farms. He vowed to "smash the *kulaks*, eliminate them as a class." Thousands of zealous Communists, supported by the secret police, fanned out into the countryside to undermine the kulaks.

A farmer who was labeled a kulak lost everything. Those who resisted faced execution or a long sentence in one of the forced-labor camps. Even many who did not resist were deported in cattle trucks and trains to Central Asia or the Siberian wilderness. Hunger and exposure killed tens of thousands along the way.

Liquidating the kulaks was only the first phase. The government took the property of individual families— land, tools, livestock, buildings—and forced them into collective farms, called *kohlkozes*. The kohlkozes were supposedly communal, but were actually highly regimented farming factories. This policy of collectivization went beyond seeds and livestock. The goal was to destroy every aspect of backward peasant culture. Work habits, folk traditions, religious faith—all of it had to be erased so that the peasants could embrace the new world of communism.

When the terrible conditions created resistance, local officials called in the Red Army. Anyone fighting back was labeled a kulak or kulak sympathizer. Facing overwhelming government force, resentful peasants on the collective farms used other tactics. Work slowdowns delayed crop deliveries, but this was minor compared to the destruction of livestock. Nearly half the horses in the Soviet Union were killed, and similar slaughters drastically thinned the population of cattle, sheep, goats, and pigs.

Stalin's own lieutenants were stunned by the strength of the resistance. The party had expected problems, but the deportation of eight million kulaks, the most productive peasants, plus the loss of vitally needed livestock, surpassed the worst predictions. Party leaders pressured Stalin to call a truce with the peasants.

Stalin saw an opportunity to turn the pressure to his advantage. On March 2, 1930, an article under his byline appeared in *Pravda*. Headlined "Dizzy With Success," the statement blamed the violence against the kulaks on overenthusiastic party officials who had lost their heads and inflicted horrors on the peasantry. Stalin's career

Peasant farm workers across Russia attempted to resist Stalin's collectivization program. (Library of Congress)

was built on dishonesty and betrayal, but this was a new level of cynicism—a blatant attempt to blame the rank and file for his own brutal mistakes. Loyal party members were caught in the middle. In order to keep up Stalin's story, government authorities had to accuse them of collectivization's mistakes, put them on trial, and punish them. In short, they suffered because they had obeyed Stalin's orders.

Stalin realized it was time to slow down forced collectivization. "Collective farms cannot be set up by force," he said. Peasants were now allowed to leave the kohlkozes and did so in droves. But they found they did not own their tools or animals and that the new farms open to them were located in swamps or wastelands. Worse, they were still expected to grow and hand over to the government impossible amounts of crops. Millions surrendered to the inevitable and returned to the kolkhozes.

Collectivization was an agricultural disaster but, unable to admit failure, Stalin again declared that all the problems were the work of kulaks and kulak sympathizers, of saboteurs, and a long list of other enemies. Stalin instructed officials to use death and deportation to deal with troublemakers. Simultaneously, Stalin pushed party workers to meet his grain quotas at all costs, even if it meant leaving no grain for the peasants to eat. This had the added benefit of starving them into submission.

No area felt the bony hand of famine more than Ukraine, a major agricultural region of the Soviet Union.

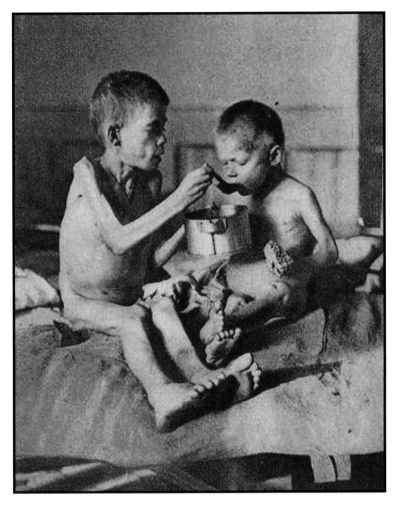

A starving boy feeds his brother during the 1932-1933 man-made famine in Ukraine. The famine was known as the Holodomor, *from the Ukrainian expression* moryty holodom, *meaning to inflict death by hunger.* (Central State Archive of Ukraine.)

Ukrainians had resisted collectivization, and Stalin knew the region had long dreamed of independence from Russia. When famine struck in 1931, Stalin and his lieutenants not only prevented relief from going to

Ukraine but also denied that people there were starving and continued to insist that Ukrainians turn over their grain.

The famine peaked in 1933—"Hungry Thirty-Three," as it came to be known. Swollen, gray-skinned farmers rummaged fields for rotted potatoes, or pillaged centuries-old graves for jewelry to trade for food. Whole villages died out. The Soviet authorities treated the victims with a heartlessness that is difficult to fathom. In one instance, a group of starving peasants were found guilty of eating a buried horse and shot. Tons of grain and potatoes rotted in the open while guards prevented hungry people from taking it. There were several reports of cannibalism.

The Ukrainian writer Miron Dolot remembered a trip to town:

> A few steps further, we saw another frozen body. It was the corpse of a woman. As I brushed away the snow, horror made my blood turn cold: under her ragged coat, clutched tightly to her bosom with her stiff hands, was the frozen little body of her baby.
>
> We finally left our village behind and stepped onto the open road which led to the county seat. . . . Everywhere we looked dead and frozen bodies lay by the sides of the road. To our right were bodies of those villagers who apparently had tried to reach the town in search of work and food. Weakened by starvation, they were unable to make it and ended up lying or falling down by the roadside.

Before the Communist government allowed the peasants to eat again, at least five million Ukrainians—roughly one in five—died. Possibly two million more perished in other regions. One Soviet official expressed the regime's priorities: "It has cost millions of lives, but the collective farm system is here to stay."

The famine did not touch Stalin or his lieutenants. They attended the theater in the winter and visited the sunny south in the summer. But death did reach into Stalin's family.

His home life had grown increasingly turbulent. The son from his first marriage, Yakov (called Yasha), was a disappointment and often a target of Stalin's ridicule. After Stalin refused his choice of a wife, Yasha tried and failed to shoot himself. "Ha!" Stalin said. "He couldn't even shoot straight."

Stalin's relationship with Nadya was also strained. She had left their two children to nannies and, on Bukharin's advice, gone to college. Still an idealist, she answered the party's call for industrial experts by studying synthetic fibers. However, her depression had worsened over the past few years. Whether this was medical, stress related, or due to despair over her marriage remains unclear. Nadya traveled to Germany to be examined by experts. Their diagnosis remains unknown, and she continued to suffer and fight with Stalin. Sometimes he hid in the bathroom while his wife screamed through the door. In the summer of 1932, Nadya left early from the family's annual vacation in the south, pleading headaches and stomach pain.

On November 8, just days after the Revolution's anniversary, the couple attended a party thrown by Klim Voroshilov, one of Stalin's inner circle. For some reason Nadya and her husband quarreled at the supper table. According to witnesses, a half-drunk Stalin flicked either orange peels or a cigarette butt at her. When she ignored him, he exclaimed, "Hey you, have a drink!"

"Don't you dare 'hey' me!" Nadya replied. As she stormed out, she screamed at Stalin to shut up.

One of the guests caught up to her outside. Nadya complained about Stalin's grumbling and his flirting with other women, and then, seemingly calm, returned home. Stalin went drinking with comrades until long after midnight and then, as usual, fell asleep in his study. Sometime during the night, Nadya shot herself. She left a note that was rumored to be full of bitter personal and political attacks on Stalin.

Stalin retreated to his room for days. "She left me as an enemy!" he cried. He drank heavily and fell into self-pity. "Never mind the children," he said. "They forgot her in a few days, but how could she do this to me?" At one point he even threatened suicide. It was left to other party leaders to organize Nadya's funeral. "I had never seen him cry," said V. I. Molotov, one of his lieutenants, "but at [her] coffin I saw tears running down his cheeks."

The newspapers said Nadya died of appendicitis. Stalin allowed his children to believe the story. For the rest of the year he went into seclusion.

No one could ever claim to know Stalin well, but those

who were around him most said Nadya's death changed him. He became even more private and occasionally morose. Most ominously, he became even more ruthless and cruel. In the coming years, several members of Nadya's family, who had made up his most intimate circle, were arrested for the flimsiest of reasons and executed.

The world outside the Soviet Union was more encouraging, however. Western capitalism was also going through a grave crisis. In 1929, the American stock market had crashed. A banking and financial crisis followed, and by 1932, the Great Depression had spread around the world, doing damage to the economies of Western Europe and elsewhere. Maybe, finally, the long-promised collapse of capitalism was on the horizon.

The average Soviet citizen, however, was too caught up in his own suffering to care about a theoretical future. Stalin's rapid industrialization and collectivization policies had created immense waste and suffering. Machinery purchased with peasant grain and peasant lives fell apart because workers were not trained to use or repair it. Factories, refineries, and other projects were started and then abandoned for lack of funds or the know-how needed to continue. Forced labor provided a significant part of the labor pool. Many of the people working on new industrial projects were kulaks, peasants, and others sentenced to work camps. Between 25,000 and 40,000 of them died digging, by hand, a canal connecting the White Sea with the Baltic Sea.

Forced labor built the Belomorekanal, *connecting the White Sea to the Baltic Sea.* (Karelian State Regional Museum, Petrozavodsk)

Thousands more ended up in the notorious gold fields in the Kolyma River region, one of the coldest places on earth. Fierce winters wiped out whole camps—inmates, guards, every living thing. These were only two of the innumerable projects conducted with what amounted to slave labor and what the Soviet government called rehabilitation.

The push for industry made some progress, though it came at a huge price in suffering. Gigantic hydroelectric works harnessed river power and factories, mines, and ironworks sprang up. Whole cities rose in the sparsely inhabited interior, many of them around industries that had not existed before.

Stalin did have the enthusiastic support of young Communist Party workers inspired by his vision of a strong, modern Soviet Union. "There are no fortresses which Bolsheviks cannot storm!" was the battle cry of a new generation. Younger people, including millions of peasants, flocked to factories and technical colleges to learn the new trades. The population's shift from the country to the cities was a huge change in Soviet society, similar to the movements of people that took place during the West's Industrial Revolution.

By 1934, Stalin was ready to declare victory. In his February speech to the party congress, which had been dubbed the "Congress of Victors," he declared unemployment abolished and poverty a thing of the past. Party leaders lined up to praise Stalin. Even Bukharin, out of a futile attempt at self-preservation, hailed Stalin as the "best of the best revolutionaries."

Stalin's "second revolution" claimed so many victims that the numbers are still debated. No one was keeping count. Low estimates start at 14.5 million. But more subtle transformation had also taken place. The failures of the early 1930s made Stalin even more suspicious and extreme. He was now willing to do anything, regardless of how cruel or wasteful, to implement Socialism In One Country and to remain in power. Terror was now a normal method of administration that soon reached into every corner of Soviet life. Stalin and his lieutenants filled the new secret police, the NKVD, with sadists and killers and fanatical Communists willing to kill, torture, and die for the cause, as well as with thousands of ordinary people needed to maintain the NKVD's system of prisons and forced-labor camps, the Gulag.

Seven
ENEMIES OF
THE PEOPLE

For much of 1934, Stalin allowed the traumatized nation a breathing spell. Cultural censorship was loosened. Once-banned plays returned to theaters, and jazz could be heard in nightclubs. Stalin's personal life reflected the relaxed atmosphere. His daughter, Svetlana, and relatives of both his late wives flocked around him. On occasion the workaholic even spent an evening watching a play or ballet or one of his favorite movies.

After being forced to make humiliating public confessions of their "errors," Zinoviev and Kamenev had been allowed back into the party, and Bukharin was editing *Izvestia* (News), one of the major Soviet newspapers. Stalin had not mellowed, however. He was merely waiting for the right moment to strike again. Meanwhile,

Although Stalin and his daughter were close when she was a child, they went through several periods of estrangement once she reached adulthood. Svetlana eventually defected to the United States in the 1960s and became a naturalized U.S. citizen. (Courtesy of Getty Images.)

NKVD agents were secretly recording his rivals' private conversations.

Spies were everywhere. In early 1934, the great poet Osip Mandelstam, a major cultural figure, read a new poem critical of Stalin to a half-dozen or so trusted listeners in a private home. On May 13, 1934, the NKVD arrested him. His wife, Nadezhda, asked for help from a number of Bolshevik figures, including Bukharin, one of the poet's admirers. Bukharin went to see Genrikh Yagoda, the head of the NKVD, to ask for Mandelstam's release. Yagoda stunned him by quoting the poem from memory. "I never saw [Bukharin] again," Nadezhda wrote later. "Later on he [said] that Yagoda had recited the poem on Stalin by heart to him, and this so frightened him he gave up his efforts." Stalin personally decided the poet's punishment and sent the Mandelstams into three years of exile.

The temporary thaw ended suddenly on December 1, 1934, when Sergei Kirov, a top lieutenant to Stalin whose popularity in the party made Stalin nervous, was assassinated by a party member named Leonid Nikolayev. Stalin rushed from Moscow with his stunned lieutenants to interrogate the assassin. Mystery surrounds what

Kirov and Stalin on vacation together in 1934, shortly before Kirov's assassination. (Novosti Photo Library, London)

happened next. One story has it that Stalin asked Nikolayev "Why?" Nikolayev pointed to NKVD officials in the room and screamed, "Why are you asking me? Ask them!" In another strange turn, Kirov's loyal bodyguard died on the way to being interrogated in what was officially reported as a truck accident. In reality, he was beaten to death by NKVD agents.

At the time, some believed Stalin ordered the assassination, either directly, or by hinting he wanted Kirov dead. Later, some historians concurred, but whether or not Stalin had a part in the crime, he certainly made sure the authorities never conducted a proper investigation. Instead he pinned the killing on a made-up terrorist organization and wrote out the list of names of the so-called terrorists to be arrested. A fair number of them, it turned out, were his old enemies.

Whatever the truth of the murder, one thing is certain. Stalin used it as an excuse to begin an era of totalitarian terror known as the Great Purge. *Purge* had a specific meaning for Bolsheviks. The Communist Party occasionally weeded out its membership to find those who failed to adapt to new directions by the party or had, for whatever reason, dropped out of active involvement. They lost their favored status and sometimes their jobs, but seldom suffered otherwise. These purges were accepted as a normal phase in the Party's development.

The Great Purge first struck at ordinary party members. Thousands lost their membership but, unlike the more benign purges of the past, most of them were also arrested for counterrevolutionary activity or other political crimes.

Each arrest put the family and friends of the accused under suspicion. The NKVD pressured them to inform on family, comrades, and coworkers. The arrest of a powerful figure snowballed into the arrests of those he had appointed or promoted or mentored.

The worst was to come. Stalin aimed his next blows at the old Bolsheviks, the veterans from the movement's earliest days. Stalin ordered Henrikh Yagoda to connect Zinoviev and Kamenev to Kirov's murder. Yagoda, although a brutal secret policeman, was also a veteran Bolshevik and knew Zinoviev and Kamenev well enough to consider the accusations absurd. Stalin, however, left no doubts about his expectations. "If you do not obtain confessions," he later said, "we will shorten you by a head."

Stalin had something special in mind for his old rivals. Theirs was to be the first of a series of show trials, public extravaganzas where the NKVD dragged the most celebrated of the old Bolsheviks into rigged trials designed to tie them to monstrous crimes. The treatment of Zinoviev and Kamenev set the pattern. First, the NKVD pressured them into confessions. Zinoviev, always weak-willed and now sick, gave in quickly. Kamenev held out until the NKVD ordered his teenaged son's arrest right in front of him. After a meeting, Zinoviev and Kamenev agreed to play along, as long as their families were protected. The accused were then rehearsed for the

Grigory Zinoviev in 1933. (Courtesy of Getty Images.)

trial, with Stalin, the prosecutors, and the NKVD con-
tributing to the script.

The Zinoviev-Kamenev show trial convened on August

19, 1936. A group of co-conspirators were tried with them. The defendants were not allowed lawyers, and the prosecutor had no evidence other than their coerced confessions. The charges spiraled into a preposterous hodgepodge of conspiracies—plots to kill Stalin, to restore capitalism, to engage in terrorism, sabotage, and assassination—all of it coming at the command of the exiled archvillain Leon Trotsky. Stalin sought to humiliate the old Bolsheviks so no one could see them as heroic martyrs. The doomed defendants implicated a long list of other prominent party members that made up the rosters for future show trials.

Stalin went back on his promise to spare their lives, and the court sentenced the defendants to death. Zinoviev and Kamenev, two of Lenin's oldest followers, were led to the execution cellars. Over the next three years, their wives, siblings, and children suffered the same fate. All were guilty of a new crime Stalin put on the books: "A member of the family of a traitor to the fatherland."

Stalin's need to destroy his rivals in such humiliating fashion perplexed many people. Bukharin, a future victim, offered one explanation. In early 1936, before the Zinoviev-Kamenev trial, he traveled to Paris on government business. There he made contact with prominent Mensheviks living in exile and took the opportunity to pass along some honest thoughts on Stalin:

> You say you don't know him well, but we do. He is unhappy at not being able to convince everyone,

himself included, that he is greater than everyone, and this unhappiness of his may be his most human trait, perhaps the only human trait in him. But what is not human, but rather devilish, is that because of this unhappiness, he cannot help taking revenge on people, on all people, but especially those who are in any way higher or better than he.

Stalin had a paranoid side to his character that intensified in the early 1930s. He often sent notes about imagined plots and conspiracies to baffled lieutenants, whose lives depended on their learning to recognize which suspicions to take seriously and which to ignore. His personal suspicion merged with his political belief that he needed to hold absolute power because he was the only person capable of completing the Marxist revolution. Any opposition to him was also treason against the revolution.

Stalin's suspicions extended to the outside world where his fears were more justified. The Western democracies remained hostile, and Fascist dictatorships that had taken power in Italy, several Eastern European countries, and most dangerously in Germany, were committed to destroying Bolshevism. The Germans, under the leadership of Adolf Hitler, had begun rearming and reindustrializing. T0heir revival constantly reminded Stalin that the USSR still lagged far behind other countries.

While there had been industrial progress, the command economy remained dysfunctional. Stalin needed scapegoats to explain away the mistakes in planning, waste, corruption, and the poor decisions inherent in a top-down economic system. Ironically, punishing the Soviet Union's economists, engineers, and technicians compounded the problems because the best engineers and scientists lived in fear or were already in the Gulag.

Stalin was not satisfied with stamping out political opposition or blaming scientists and engineers for the country's economic failures. He also took aim at the Soviet Union's spiritual and cultural life. He meant to rebuild the USSR's art and intellect according to his own tastes and his interpretation of what a Marxist society needed.

"Soviet literature should be able to portray our heroes; it should be able to glimpse our tomorrow," one of Stalin's lieutenants said. The titles of a few works of the time make it clear that the workers—and Stalin—were to be society's heroes: *The Big Conveyor Belt, Grain, I, A Son of the Working People*, and *Lenin in October*, the last a film starring the actor playing Stalin. All art required government approval. Approved topics included workers, Stalin, collectivization, industrialization, and Lenin. The heroes of books and film lived their lives and performed their deeds guided by the wisdom of Comrade Stalin—leader, teacher, and father. Writers took to imitating Stalin's bland prose style, while Stalin's love of traditional folk music brought harp-playing ancients from the farthest corners of the USSR to Moscow.

Stalin actively created a celebrity cult. Reports, scholarly texts, and novels came with a preamble celebrating and quoting the leader. Schoolchildren chanted, "Thank you, Comrade Stalin, for our happy childhood!" When Stalin officially celebrated his sixtieth birthday in 1939, *Pravda* turned over five of its six pages to tell Stalin's life story and for months printed some of the thousands of tributes that came in from around the country.

At the beginning of 1937, the purges entered a new, bloodier phase. That January's show trial featured Georgy Pyatakov, one of the masterminds of rapid industrialization and one of the foremost scapegoats for the economic setbacks. Pyatakov was a deputy to Sergo Orzhonikidze, a popular Bolshevik leaders and Stalin's friend and comrade for thirty years. After the trial, Stalin broke another promise and ordered Pyatakov's execution. Orzhonikidze confronted him. "Koba, why do you let the NKVD arrest my men without informing me? . . . I demand that this authoritarianism cease!"

In the middle of February, Stalin and Orzhonikidze had a long talk behind closed doors. Orzhonikidze was dead the next afternoon. When he heard the news, Stalin exclaimed, "Heavens, what a tricky illness! The chap lay down to have a rest and the result was a fit and a heart attack." In fact, Orzhonikidze died of gunshot wound, probably forced into suicide by the NKVD.

Five days later, Bukharin and one of his political partners, Alexei Rykov, appeared before selected members of the Central Committee. The pair sat silently as Stalin's lieutenants outdid one another with wild accusations against them. Stalin said little, as was usual for

One of the most powerful ways in which Stalin created the cult of personality that surrounded him was through art. Soviet painters of the socialist realism school produced hundreds of portraits glorifying party leaders. This 1939 portrait, evoking a kindly school-master image of Stalin, was painted by Aleksandr Gerasimov, who was, in effect, Stalin's court painter. (State Tretyakov Gallery, Moscow)

him in such situations. Bukharin rejected the charges and added, "I am not Zinoviev or Kamenev, and I will not tell lies against myself."

Stalin let the pair stew before summoning them a few days later. Both men left home that morning knowing they would never see their families again. The NKVD seized Bukharin and Rykov during the meeting and took them straight to the Lubyanka, the notorious prison a short distance away.

Not even the secret police were safe. Soon after the Bukharin-Rykov arrests, Stalin charged the NKVD with allowing so many conspiracies to take place. Yagoda was arrested, and several secret police operatives in his entourage committed suicide or were marched straight into execution cells.

Stalin had a new man in mind as head of the NKVD. Nikolai Yezhov had led the Kirov investigation and the Zinoviev-Kamenev frame-up. Yezhov was a popular party member, modest and charming, often singing and playing guitar at social functions. He was also a murderer and an alcoholic.

The oppression entered a new phase that came to be called the Great Terror. An old secret-police saying— "Give us a man, and we'll make a case"—was appropriated by the NKVD and applied with a vengeance. The list of crimes that could get one executed was almost endless. Any association with a disgraced old Bolshevik made one a Zinovievist or, most deadly of all, a Trotskyist. To be religious, regardless of the faith, was risky. Russian Orthodox priests, Jehovah's Witnesses, and Muslims back from Mecca: all were arrested. Travel abroad was suspicious, as was having friends, relatives, or colleagues in other countries. The system became ever more absurd and tragic. To speak Esperanto was to be an enemy of the people; to have owned a hotel before the Revolution could mean doom; work for the Red Cross led to arrest. Soviet citizens denounced stamp collectors as foreign spies, and meteorologists were shot for bad weather forecasts. In one case, a textile worker was arrested for sabotage when he made the pockets of some pants too small.

Stalin set up a quota system for arrests. Each town or city or collective farm provided a specified number of saboteurs or Trotskyists. Failure to fill the quota was not an option, unless an official wanted to be shot. The circumstances of a case didn't matter. A legal system governed by "Give us a man, and we'll make a case" had no need for concepts such as evidence and motive.

Stalin struck especially hard at the intelligentsia. He had already imposed his own tastes on music, art, film, and literature. The terror now forced science to conform. Theories cooked up by Stalin-approved cranks replaced legitimate research. Meanwhile, the elite in engineering, aeronautics, and physics were sent to special gulags to continue their work while a generation of engineers and technicians faced extinction.

All along, Stalin pretended to be unaware of the NKVD's actions. In his speeches he kept demanding that the secret police obey the law and even professed to fear the NKVD might arrest him. This fed the myth of Stalin as a benevolent ruler surrounded by evil men, which led worldly writers, hard-hearted Communists, and tortured innocents to exclaim on occasion, "If only Stalin knew about this!"

Stalin, of course, knew and participated at every level of the Great Terror. Sentencing people to die was part of his work day. Records show his signature on execution lists with thousands of names. His lieutenant Molotov had similar powers, as did Yezhov and others in the inner circle. None of them had the least interest in a case's details. Yezhov once sent Stalin a list with the request, "For eventual arrest: to be verified."

Stalin simply replied, "Don't verify. Arrest."

He turned the terror on the military as well. The press informed a stunned nation that Mikhail Tukhachevsky, the most renowned of the Red Army generals and a hero of the civil war, had been shot for treason. Forensic tests conducted years later found his written confession spattered with blood. Secret trials condemned almost the entire high command to death. Over 36,000 officers were swept away. With the destruction of the officer corps, Stalin believed he had eliminated the one group still capable of overthrowing him. During World War II, his country would pay a heavy price for his peace of mind.

The last of the big show trials began March 2, 1938. Joining Bukharin in the dock were Rykov and Yagoda, the ex-NKVD boss, plus eighteen others. The prosecution resurrected all the old conspiracies and ridiculous charges, but also added some new wrinkles—that Yagoda had tried to poison Yezhov and, the biggest blockbuster of all, that Bukharin had attempted to kill Lenin and Stalin in 1918.

It is believed Stalin attended some of the trial. (Officials had wired the courtroom to allow Stalin to listen in from his office.) As it turned out, the show provided more drama than expected. The defendants admitted to their part in a vast anti-Stalin conspiracy, but Bukharin

A native of St. Petersburg, Nikolai Yezhov joined the Bolsheviks shortly before the October Revolution and became one of Stalin's most loyal followers and the head of the NKVD during the great purge. By 1939, Yezhov had fallen out of Stalin's favor and was tried and executed for espionage and treason, as well as homosexuality. (Library of Congress)

used double-talk, evasiveness, and stubbornness to deny or undermine specific charges. The tactic required subtlety. The NKVD had not tortured him, but they made it clear the lives of his wife and infant son depended on his performance. Yet his defiance did not matter in the end. Stalin had passed judgment before the trial began. Just before his execution, Bukharin penned a quick note to his adversary. "Koba," he asked, "why do you need me to die?" Two days later, the government announced the executions.

Yezhov, meanwhile, had begun to break down. Always sickly, his heavy drinking drove him into a deep depression. After the Bukharin trial, he was ordered to kill his protégés in the NKVD, a sure sign that he was on his way to becoming an enemy of the people. Other members of the leadership, sensing a change in Stalin's feelings, now began to speak out against the NKVD boss. He was accused of taking the terror too far and was assigned an assistant, an enthusiastic Georgian named Lavrenti Beria, who immediately began to eliminate Yezhov's followers.

Trained as an architect, Beria had made his name as a secret policeman in his native Georgia. Bald, smallish, often in spectacles or a pince-nez, he did not, at first glance, appear to be what he was—a sexual predator and sadist who liked to personally torture prisoners. Beria was an efficient administrator of terror. His statement, "You're a good worker but if you'd served six years in the camps, you'd work even better," expressed his management philosophy.

In early December, Beria officially replaced his superior. When the NKVD shot Yezhov in 1940, the government did not bother to announce his execution. By one estimate 23,000 NKVD agents died around the same time. Killing the killers guaranteed they would remain silent about the crimes they had committed.

Yezhov's fall coincided with Stalin's easing of the terror. The NKVD had warned him that the terror machine was choking on the sheer number of people that had been arrested, jailed, or executed.

Stalin, usually never shy about his accomplishments, dubbed this bloody period as the "Time of Yezhov," rather than the more appropriate "Time of Stalin." He used Yezhov's fall to add to the myth of "If only Stalin knew about this!" He released 327,000 prisoners to give the impression of sweeping in to save innocent victims. Years later he was still keeping up the charade.

Having physically destroyed his enemies, Stalin ordered the party to erase them from history. Stalin's book *The Short Course*, published under his supervision as the official textbook on Soviet history, reduced the most important figures of the Revolution, except Lenin, to a bunch of spies and traitors, when it mentioned them at all. Party officials dug up and destroyed books, articles, speeches, and essays written by the old Bolsheviks. For the ordinary citizen, owning any work by these enemies of the people invited arrest. Party zealots airbrushed former Politburo members from photographs, scribbled over the faces of war heroes with pens, or cut them out of the picture with scissors and razor blades.

Later, discussing the Great Terror, Stalin admitted to "grave mistakes . . . more mistakes than might have been expected. . . . Nevertheless, the Purge of 1933-36 was unavoidable and its results, on the whole, were beneficial." He noticeably failed to mention the terror of 1937-38. As with the other catastrophes of the Stalin years, statistics about the Great Terror are still uncertain. It is known there were days the NKVD killed over one thousand people in Moscow alone. According to one source, there were 353,680 death sentences in 1937. This does not count the millions sent to prisons or gulags.

Stalin had one more old enemy to get rid of though, the most dangerous and pernicious of them all. Trotsky had fled to Mexico City. There, on August 20, 1940, as he worked on a biography of Stalin, an NKVD agent posing as an admirer murdered him by driving a metal ice pick into his head.

Eight

THE ROAD TO TOTAL WAR

As the 1930s neared its end, Stalin had to focus most of his attention on the outside world. Another European war began to appear inevitable. Nazi Germany had absorbed Austria, seized Czechoslovakia, and now threatened Poland, an ally of Britain and France. By the summer of 1939, Stalin's days and nights were full of diplomatic maneuvers, hidden talks, and secret deals.

Adolf Hitler's regime in Germany was rabidly anti-Communist. Hitler had even merged his notorious anti-Semitism with anticommunism. He frequently railed against "Jewish-Bolshevism" in his speeches and writings. Hitler's own autobiography, *Mein Kampf,* written before he seized power, made it clear he intended to cleanse the world of Soviet communism, conquer

Russia, and turn its so-called subhuman Slavic inhabitants into slaves.

France and Great Britain's hostility to the USSR extended back to the October Revolution. Both countries had sent troops and supplies to support the White armies in the Civil War. Although the United States officially recognized the Soviet Union in the early 1930s, the Roosevelt Administration was cool toward Stalin. Only France warmed slightly toward the USSR as the German threat grew.

Always suspicious, Stalin gathered information on other nations both officially and through espionage. He did not favor one side or the other. The fascist Germans and democratic British and French were all capitalist regimes. That they were in conflict was a natural consequence of dying capitalism. Lenin had said—and Stalin agreed—that capitalist states would always fight wars. Lenin had also insisted that the Soviet state should never get mixed up in these conflicts. Better to let the capitalist nations destroy one another.

Yet, Stalin recognized that a European war posed a threat to the Soviet Union; it would not be able to remain neutral. But the Great Terror had crippled the Red Army, and Soviet industry could not produce the necessary weapons, vehicles, or other war material.

As war approached, Stalin had two interlocking goals: stall for time and prepare for war. He took charge of foreign policy and appointed his closest lieutenant, V. I. Molotov, as head of foreign affairs. The two shared a

Meeting of the Central Committee of the Soviet Communist Party in 1939. Stalin stands in the center. Vyacheslav Molotov, Stalin's chief advisor during the war, sits to Stalin's left. (Courtesy of Art Resource.)

long history. When Stalin arrived in Petrograd in 1917, Molotov stepped aside as editor of *Pravda*. A few years later, he was Stalin's predecessor as general secretary and eventually rose to be Stalin's right-hand man in the 1920s. Thereafter he was involved in all Politburo matters, from economic decisions to mass murder.

Molotov was known for his blandness and lack of imagination—Trotsky and Bukharin had called him a blockhead. But Stalin respected Molotov's work habits. He was nicknamed "Iron Butt" for his ability to work at his desk for hours on end. Molotov also had an artistic side. He played violin and mandolin, and Stalin often sang while Molotov accompanied him on piano, one of the Soviet leader's favorite pastimes. When Stalin went into seclusion after Nadya's death, Molotov was one of the few allowed to see him. His loyalty to Stalin was so solid that when Stalin sent Molotov's wife to the Gulag after World War II, Molotov divorced her without complaining.

On August 3, 1939, in a move that would eventually shock the world, Germany secretly contacted the Soviet government seeking a treaty of nonaggression. Hitler had decided to invade Poland. Though Poland was allied with Britain and France, Hitler did not think they would go to war for the Poles, especially if they had no chance of making Stalin an ally. Keeping the USSR neutral was an essential part of his strategy.

After receiving the German feeler, Stalin played it cool for sixteen days. He met with British and French representatives to hear their offer. But, foolishly, with time short and so much at stake, those nations did not even bother to send high-level officials. The representatives that arrived on a slow steamship lacked the power to finalize an agreement. "They're not being serious," Stalin said.

In the meantime, Hitler broke through Stalin's aloofness with a personal note that proved his seriousness. Secret talks were arranged, and shortly after the British delegation left Moscow, Germany's foreign minister, Joachim von Ribbentrop, arrived. The talks moved quickly, and on the night of August 23, the two dictatorships signed an agreement promising not to attack each other. In an added secret protocol, Hitler and Stalin agreed to carve up Poland, Hitler the west and Stalin the east. In addition, this so-called Pact of Steel granted that Estonia, Latvia, and Finland were in the USSR's "sphere of influence," while Poland and Lithuania fell within Germany's.

Hearing of the deal, Hitler exclaimed, "I have them! I have them!" Stalin celebrated with his cronies on a duck-hunting trip in the country. "Of course it's all a game of who can fool whom," he told them. "I know what Hitler's up to. He thinks he's outsmarted me but actually it's I who's tricked him."

The Nazi-Soviet Pact sealed Poland's fate. From the Soviet point of view, the pact steered German aggression away from the Soviet Union and toward the West. If the Poles tied up the Germans for several months—a widely held assumption in Europe—and the Anglo-French alliance fought Germany as fiercely as they had in World War I in the West, the Soviet Union would hopefully have two years, maybe more, to strengthen itself before Germany turned on it.

Hitler turned loose the blitzkrieg against Poland on September 1. Britain and France declared war two days later. Then Stalin got his first shock. Poland fell in only three weeks. Stalin had to scramble to grab the piece of the country promised in the pact. He justified the Soviet invasion publicly by claiming he wished to protect Ukrainians and Belarussians living inside the Polish borders. He, and many of his countrymen, thought those areas had been unfairly awarded to Poland after World

WONDER HOW LONG THE HONEYMOON WILL LAST?

This American cartoon from October 1939 examines the Nazi-Soviet nonaggression pact with skepticism. (Library of Congress)

War I, when Lenin's government was too weak to fight back.

Later that month Hitler sent Foreign Minister Ribbentrop to Moscow to work out the final details of Poland's division. Stalin, having reclaimed the areas he wanted, swapped the rest of his share in return for having Lithuania included in the Soviet sphere of influence. The countries also worked out a trade agreement. The Soviet Union would supply raw materials—grain, oil, ore—in return for German technology and manufactured goods, including sophisticated military material.

Stalin went out of his way to declare himself Germany's great friend. "The friendship of the peoples of Germany and the Soviet Union," he said in a telegram to Hitler, "cemented by blood, has every reason to be lasting and firm."

At the same time, Stalin prepared for war. If the Germans marched east, he now had part of Poland as a buffer zone. But the situation looked bad elsewhere. Lithuania was, both culturally and politically, close to Germany. Finland was an even softer spot in his defenses. The Finnish border was within striking distance of Petrograd, now called Leningrad, a serious threat because the Finnish government was close to Germany. Stalin demanded that Finland give up territory the Soviet Union needed to defend itself. When the Finns refused, Stalin ordered the Red Army to attack.

The Red Army predicted victory in days, but the Finnish forces, well-armed and trained to fight in winter conditions, held out ten weeks. Stalin now paid the price for slaughtering the Red Army's officer corps and putting his cronies in charge of the military. One of them, G. I. Kulik, thought horses preferable to mechanical vehicles. Another, Lev Mekhlis, had far more experience purging armies than leading them. Kliment Voroshilov, the commissar of defense, was a notorious incompetent. Finally, far superior Soviet numbers and artillery defeated the Finns, but at the cost of at least 120,000—perhaps as many as 200,000—Red Army lives.

Most damaging, the confrontation had revealed the Soviet Union's military weakness.

After a lull, Hitler returned to the offensive the following April. If Poland's quick defeat surprised Stalin, the rapid collapse of the western front left him stunned in disbelief. In just over three months, the Germans occupied Denmark and Norway, rolled over the Netherlands and Belgium, forced the British to evacuate the European continent, and defeated France. So much for the two years Stalin thought he was buying in the Hitler pact. "Couldn't they put up any resistance at all?" he asked.

Stalin needed to bulk up Soviet defenses, and saw the best chance to do so by extending his border into the lands of the old czarist empire that Lenin had given up to get out of World War I. The Soviets ordered Estonia, Latvia, and Lithuania to allow Red Army troops inside their borders for so-called defensive purposes. All were too small and weak to disobey. The NKVD came in behind the Red Army and unleashed all the familiar horrors of collectivization and mass terror. Russian colonists soon arrived to take the homes and jobs of displaced and liquidated Estonians, Latvians, and Lithuanians.

Stalin's suspicions of other national groups within the Soviet Union intensified. The Finns living north of Leningrad, German speakers in the Volga River region, Chinese and Korean communities in the east, and others were uprooted and deported to remote areas.

Meanwhile, tension between Germany and the USSR increased over dividing Eastern Europe. Stalin had hoped to expand Soviet control. The Nazi regime had more influence with the Fascist governments of the area however, and both Hungary and Romania joined Germany's list of allies. More ominously, German troops had taken up positions in Romania and Finland, on the Soviet border. Stalin sent Molotov to Berlin, but little came of

The Soviet border would shift dramatically during World War II, moving as far east as the green line and as far west as the blue line.

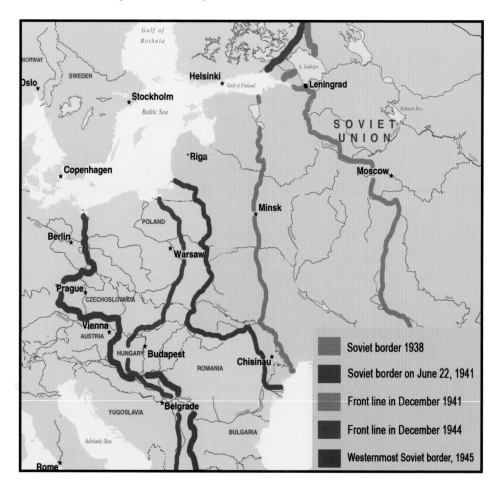

Soviet border 1938

Soviet border on June 22, 1941

Front line in December 1941

Front line in December 1944

Westernmost Soviet border, 1945

the talks. Hitler always intended to attack Russia some day, but Stalin's insistence on having a say in Eastern European affairs may have hurried his timeline. On December 18, 1940, the German dictator approved plans for the invasion of Russia, code-named *Barbarossa*.

Facing the danger of a two-front war, with Germany to the west and its Axis ally Japan to the east, Stalin did score one diplomatic victory. The Soviets had watched with growing concern the Japanese invasion of the Chinese province of Manchuria in 1931. The two countries had even fought briefly along the Soviet-Chinese frontier in 1939. Under pressure, Stalin and Molotov, with the help of a lot of champagne, negotiated a neutrality agreement with the Japanese foreign minister. The bargaining was tough—at one point Stalin theatrically clutched at his throat as if to say, "You're choking me," but they finally reached a settlement. Stalin was free from the threat of a Japanese attack in Asia. The Japanese, in turn, could plan for war with the U.S. in the Pacific without worrying about a Soviet attack.

Now Stalin entered into one of the strangest periods of his career. Despite pleas from his generals, he refused to plan for the German invasion. Reports of German troops near the Soviet border did not faze him. Troop buildups had, after all, preceded Hitler's demands in the past. Stalin was determined to give up whatever Hitler demanded, if it would delay an attack. General Georgi Zhukov, the Soviet Union's most successful military leader in the coming war, said Stalin's "entire thoughts and actions were based on a single desire—to avoid war or delay its outbreak, which he was certain he could achieve."

Warnings kept pouring in—from spies, from the British, from Soviet observers. Even Germany's ambassador to the Soviet Union, who secretly opposed the German invasion, leaked the date of the attack. Stalin refused to listen. He ordered the military to ignore the German planes in Soviet airspace and the troops on its border. They were provocations, he said, trying to entice him to make the first move.

Then, on June 22, 1941, at 3:15 AM, just before dawn of the longest day of the year, Hitler unleashed Operation Barbarossa on the Soviet Union.

As the first reports came in from the front, General Zhukov convinced a bodyguard to awaken Stalin. Once Stalin came to the phone, Zhukov "reported the situation and requested permission to start retaliation. Stalin was silent. The only thing I could hear was the sound of his breathing.

"'Do you understand me?'

"Silence again."

When Stalin finally found his voice, he refused to give Zhukov the orders he requested and instead ordered an emergency Politburo meeting, during which he sat, pale, playing with his pipe. He continued to ignore pleas from his military, still insisting that it was a provocation by renegade German generals. "Hitler surely does not know about it," he added.

Hitler knew. An army of three million Germans, along with 900,000 auxiliary troops, had swept into the Soviet Union. Germans bombers were in the process of destroying most of the Soviet air force on the ground. Whole Soviet armies were being annihilated or surrounded all along the front.

For the next six days, Stalin alternated between rage and deepening depression. "Stalin said, 'We blew it,'" Molotov later recalled. "This referred to all of us. I remember it well; he simply said, 'We blew it.' Yes, we blew it. Such a troubled state was Stalin in then. I tried to cheer him up a bit."

On July 3, Stalin at last spoke via radio to his staggered nation. He began with the lie that Germany's best troops had been destroyed. He justified the pact with Hitler as allowing the USSR much-needed time. And he asked for ruthlessness toward the Germans and for "cowards, for panic-mongerers and deserters" on the Soviet side. Before he finished, he gave an order to scorch the earth:

> The collective farmers must drive all their cattle and turn over their grain . . . for transportation to the rear. All valuable property, including metals, grain, and fuel . . . must be destroyed without fail. . . . [S]abotage groups must be organized to combat the enemy, to foment guerilla warfare, blow up bridges and roads, damage telephone and telegraph lines, set fire to forests, stores, and transport. . . . [The enemy] must be hounded and annihilated at every step.

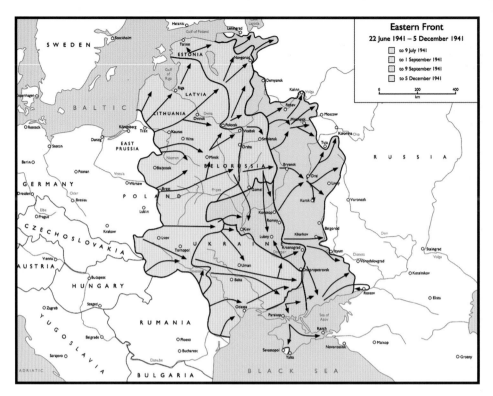

Operation Barbarossa: the Nazi invasion of the Soviet Union from June 1941 through December 1941.

Gone was the typical Marxist scorn for nationalism and patriotism. The front page of *Pravda* declared this to be "The Great Patriotic War." Soviet citizens responded to the plea to save Russia. Millions joined poorly armed units to be sent into combat and slaughtered by the German army. Over 11,000 military officers were recalled from prison and the Gulag.

The Soviet losses were catastrophic. Prisoners of war numbered in the hundreds of thousands, soon in the millions. By early October, the German blitzkrieg was within striking distance of Moscow. Stalin summoned Zhukov to take command of the city's defense. Muscovites burned official documents and Communist Party

This propaganda poster during the Nazi invasion of the Soviet Union says, "Soldier of the Red Army, save us!" (Library of Congress)

cards. Stores were looted; people fled the capital with whatever they could carry. As the Germans neared, Stalin ordered the government to evacuate. For a time it was unclear whether or not he had gone with them. But when the government announced that Stalin meant to stay, the worst of the panic passed.

Stalin made his willingness to stand and fight to the bloody end into a grand gesture. On November 7, he watched the traditional Red Square parade in honor of the revolution from atop Lenin's Mausoleum. The boom of artillery echoed on the city's borders. The ordered lines of soldiers and militia passing before him marched straight to the nearby front.

The Germans made an attempt to take the city on November 15, pushing the Soviets back. "Are you sure we'll be able to hold Moscow?" Stalin asked Zhukov, adding, "It hurts me to ask you that. Answer me truthfully, as a Communist."

But by then, Russia's traditional ally, the weather, had come to its defense. Snow fell earlier than it had in years, and mud and slush slowed the tanks and trucks of the German blitzkrieg. German soldiers, clad only in their summer uniforms, were forced to steal peasant clothes and stuff their boots with straw. Battles took place in waist-deep snow, with both sides exhausted and battered by temperatures that plunged to minus-forty degrees Celsius.

On December 5, the German generals called a halt to the attack. The same day, the Soviets counterattacked, using forces that had been stationed along the Soviet-Chinese border. These troops were available because of the neutrality agreement signed between Russia and Japan in the spring, just a few months before. This time, the exhausted Germans fell back. By the end of the year the Red Army had pushed the front line safely away from the capital.

Nine

AN UNEASY ALLIANCE

During the war, Stalin usually worked at the Kremlin, the giant building in Moscow that housed the Soviet government, from the afternoon into the early morning hours, near a bank of telephones and a telegraph room. Field commanders reported to him twice a day. Failure to check in risked his wrath. The day's visitors waiting in a lobby outside his office gave up their pistols before entering, even the generals. Once admitted, a visitor gave his report in a brisk manner and left, unless Stalin asked questions. Stalin often paced as he listened, puffing his pipe or stuffing it with tobacco from broken up cigarettes. Long explanations exasperated him, as did attempts to hedge an opinion. If he put down his pipe, an eruption of his temper was coming. His amazing

Stalin strolls the grounds at the Kremlin, accompanied by Kliment Voroshilov, one of the commanders of the Red Army. Voroshilov outlived Stalin by sixteen years and remained a prominent figure in the party under both Khrushchev and Brezhnev. (State Tretyakov Gallery, Moscow)

memory allowed him to keep of track military, industrial, and diplomatic matters in detail. He learned fast and worked incredibly hard for a man in his mid-sixties. Four-teen hour days were common; many ran to sixteen or eighteen.

After working late into the night, he usually returned to Kuntsevo, his home outside the city, to amenities such as modern bathrooms, a goldfish tank, and an air raid shelter reached by elevator. He liked to read history until he dropped off to sleep, as often as not still in his clothes.

Despite his work ethic, Stalin's personality was an obstacle to effective war leadership. He remained suspicious and, in the early years of the war, made impossible demands. When commanders fell short of his expectations, he dispatched one of his lieutenants to whip them into shape. Inevitably, the visits caused greater confusion. Stalin often called commanders in the middle of a battle with orders distracting them from the ongoing chaos of war. The Red Army had to overcome problems with training, morale, and leadership, and industry remained unable to supply the army.

After failing to take Moscow, Hitler concentrated his attacks on the south, the center of Soviet agriculture, coal, and oil production. In a matter of weeks, the German Army smashed through Ukraine. When Stalin and Nikita Khrushchev, who would become the leader of the Soviet Union after Stalin's death, mismanaged the retreat from the city of Kharkov, it cost the Red Army 250,000 captured soldiers. By late summer, one wing of the German Army had reached the Caucasus Mountains. Another threatened Stalingrad, formerly Tsaritsyn, the site of Stalin's civil war triumphs and the gate to defending the Soviet oil fields on the Caspian Sea.

Furious at the defeats, and unable to admit his part in the disaster, Stalin released a wave of terror against the armed forces. He had already scapegoated the commanders during the initial invasion. Several had been tortured as traitors, and their replacements were threatened with the same fate if they failed. As for ordinary soldiers, retreat or surrender—even under hopeless circumstances—was now considered treason. Already burdened with bad commanders and scanty equipment, they were marched into enemy fire, often unarmed, with their own officers ready to shoot them in the back if they hesitated. Stalin did not spare their families. A new order, "Not One Step Backwards," added another terrible dimension to soldiers' lives. It said, "All service personnel taken prisoner are declared outside the law and their families are subject to punishment." Soldiers taken captive were written off as dead men by the Soviet regime—there would be no trades for prisoners of war.

That same summer Stalin reopened diplomacy with the West. The German attack had thrown the Soviet Union into an automatic, if uneasy, alliance with Great Britain and the United States, which had entered the war after the Japanese attack on the Pearl Harbor naval base on December 7, 1941. The new Allies made arrangements to ship war material to the Soviets. On August 12, 1942, Britain's fiercely anti-Communist prime minister, Winston Churchill, arrived in Moscow for talks. These two men, both long committed to the other's destruction, now had to form a partnership to save their countries.

Churchill brought bad news: the Allies could not open a second front in Europe to take pressure off the Soviets. Stalin was angry at what he called a broken promise. Over the next three days, the leaders exchanged blunt language. Stalin insulted British honor, and a

furious Churchill blustered and paced the floor at his guest villa. An immense nineteen-course dinner failed to improve his mood.

Stalin needed American and British supplies, but more than anything he wanted a second front to drain troops from Hitler's attacks on the USSR. He maintained his belief that Great Britain and the U.S. intended to let the Nazis and Communists bleed each another to death. He also feared the democracies would make a separate peace with Germany. Churchill insisted the two countries simply lacked the men and equipment to invade Europe in 1942. The tension grew so bad

Churchill prepared to leave for home without the alliance solidified.

The night before Churchill's departure, Stalin made a gesture to salvage the situation. "You are leaving at daybreak," he said. "Why should we not go to my house and have some drinks?"

"I replied that I was in principle always in favor of such a policy," Churchill wrote later. Drinks turned into a relaxed dinner. While little was resolved, the two leaders did have a chance to connect. Both talked about their redheaded daughters, and Stalin even called in Svetlana to show her off. Dinner ended around 3:00 AM and Churchill departed in better spirits, convinced they could work together.

Eventually a few of Stalin's entourage began to make positive contributions to the war effort. Lavrenti Beria, who had been given control of industry as well as the NKVD, showed a knack for getting the economy back on its feet. But most of Stalin's lieutenants were incompetent on the battlefield. He approached Zhukov to become supreme battlefield commander, but the general hesitated.

"My character wouldn't let us work together," he said.

"Disaster threatens the country," Stalin replied. "We must save the Motherland by every possible means, no matter the sacrifice. What of our characters? Let's subordinate them to the interest of the Motherland."

Stalin had won Zhukov over. Stalin also appointed military men to important posts and allowed them

leeway to make suggestions and, as importantly, disagree with him, albeit within limits.

During the autumn and early winter of 1942, the
focus was on Stalingrad. The two huge German and
Soviet military machines were reduced to fighting bloody
battles for single buildings, in some cases single rooms.
In mid-November, the Soviets released an enormous
counterattack of a million soldiers and 1,400 tanks that
surrounded the elite German Sixth Army. At the end of
February 1943, the Germans surrendered. The Soviet
victory at Stalingrad changed the course of the war.

*Operation Blue: Hitler's advance on the Soviet Union from May 1942 through
November 1942.*

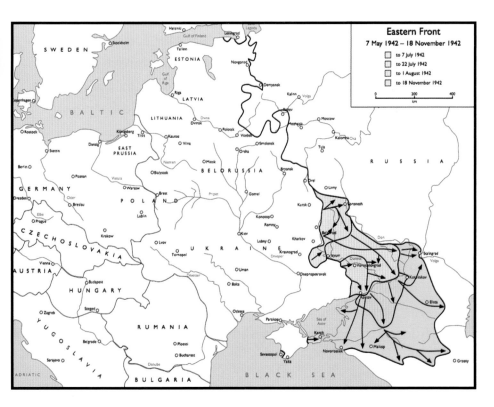

From then on, the Red Army steadily pushed the Germans to the west, toward Berlin.

Around the same time, in April 1943, Stalin's son Yakov killed himself in a German POW camp. He had been captured in the early days of the war, much to Stalin's humiliation. Under the "Not One Step Backwards" order, Yakov's wife was sent to prison. Only after the war did Stalin learn the real story of his son's death. Yakov—so often put down, so unloved and scorned—had resisted pressure to cooperate with the Germans. Stalin read the transcript of his son's interrogation that ended, "I don't know how I could face my father. I'm ashamed to be alive."

In November, Stalin, Churchill, and American president Franklin Delano Roosevelt met for a summit conference at Teheran, Iran. Stalin had resisted the conference for some time, insisting he could not leave the Soviet Union. When meetings were held in other countries, he sent Molotov to represent him. But Teheran was close enough to the Soviet borders for Stalin to travel by train.

During the Teheran meetings, Stalin came across as unshakable, quick to grasp the Allies' strategies. He seemed relaxed, smoking and doodling here, trading jabs with Churchill there. As one British official put it, "Never once in his statements did he make any strategic error, nor did he ever fail to appreciate all the implications of a situation with a quick and unerring eye." He was blunt with his demands, yet worked to charm Roosevelt and ease Churchill's suspicions about Soviet intentions. All three leaders agreed that Germany had caused enough trouble in the past thirty years and discussed breaking up the country after the war. Stalin, along with some of Roosevelt's staff, wanted to strip Germany of its industry, but no final decision on Germany's future was made.

More controversial was Stalin's insistence on keeping the USSR's borders as they had been in 1941—after the Soviet Union absorbed Lithuania, Latvia, Estonia, and parts of Poland and Romania. Neither Britain nor the United States approved of Stalin's demand, but both recognized that the middle of a world war was not the time to get into the dispute—with one exception.

Churchill, and to a lesser extent Roosevelt, considered Poland a separate case from the other areas. Great Britain had gone to war over Poland, and Churchill felt it his duty to defend it. Over dinner, he proposed that country's borders be moved west—into German territory—to compensate for the loss of eastern Poland to the Soviet Union. Stalin hedged at first but later expressed interest.

More than territory was at issue for Stalin. In the war's early days, over 21,000 Polish officers had fallen into Soviet hands. The NKVD had executed them and dumped the bodies into mass graves in Katyn Forest. When the Germans discovered the remains of the Katyn Massacre, Stalin had blamed Nazi executioners for the crime. At the time, it was easy to assign guilt to the Germans, considering the atrocities they were committing elsewhere. But if the evidence was reappraised, it would become evident that Soviets, not Germans, had killed the unarmed prisoners.

Poland was only part of the larger question. The Allied leaders realized that once Germany was defeated, they would have to make decisions that affected all of Eastern Europe. Stalin, in demanding the 1941 borders, was asking for territory that had belonged to the Russian Empire. But his ambitions did not stop there; he saw all of Eastern Europe as an opportunity. By setting up puppet governments, he could build a buffer around the USSR and spread communism. Socialism In One Country had been imposed on him by Soviet weakness. The new, victorious USSR would have the strength and opportunity to expand.

As Stalin revived Russia's imperial dreams, Churchill, still an anti-Communist to the core, worked to foil his ambitions. The clash came into the open as the conference continued. During strategy discussions, Churchill pushed hard for an invasion of the Balkan Peninsula to precede an invasion of France, which would open up the long-delayed second front. No doubt Stalin grasped Churchill's ulterior motive—if Allied troops landed in Eastern Europe, they, rather than the Red Army, would liberate those countries and control their futures. The invasion of France had to come next, Stalin insisted. American, and even some British, military leaders agreed. In a follow-up discussion Stalin further angered Churchill when he asked if the British believed in Operation Overlord (the planned invasion of France at Normandy) or if they simply talked about it to reassure the Russians.

Roosevelt eventually sided with Stalin. He wanted to win the war as soon as possible and to secure Soviet help against the Japanese in the Far East. This meant more to him than the fate of Eastern Europe after the war. The Allies, over Churchill's objections, agreed to invade France the following year. Stalin had his second front.

The 1944 campaigns pushed the German army almost entirely out of the Soviet Union. By now Soviet industry was outproducing Germany and had caught up to Britain. Huge amounts of material continued to arrive from the U.S., fulfilling its promise to supply the Soviet war effort. And then in June, the Normandy invasion opened up the long-desired second front.

Churchill visited Moscow again that October, and the future of Eastern Europe was at the top of the agenda. A strange agreement came out of the talks, one Churchill regretted almost immediately. In essence, the two powers agreed to divide up influence in each country. For instance, the Soviets received between 75-90 percent of the influence in Romania and Bulgaria; the two sides split Yugoslavia and Hungary 50-50; and the British had 90 percent of the influence in Greece. "It was all settled in no more time than it takes to sit down," Churchill remembered. Few details were written down—Churchill knew carving up other people's countries was bound to look bad. (He called the original proposal with the percentages the "naughty document.") Nor did the two

From left to right: *Winston Churchill, Franklin Roosevelt, and Joseph Stalin during the Yalta Conference. Stalin's aloof demeanor is evident in this famous photograph. Although Yalta is considered the high point in the alliance between the "Big Three" world powers, it also can be seen as the beginning of the Cold War.* (National Archives)

leaders establish what they meant by "influence." It did not ultimately matter. After the war, the Soviet Union took 100 percent of most of the countries in its sphere.

In February 1945, Stalin, Roosevelt, and Churchill met again at Yalta, a war-ravaged resort city in southern Russia. All of the participants arrived knowing Allied victory was certain. The issues discussed at Yalta were complex and the talks were full of bickering, controversy, and secrecy.

Stalin asked for territory in Asia lost by the czar in the 1905 war. Roosevelt signed a secret agreement granting him the Asian areas in return for Stalin's promise to declare war on Japan.

The issue of Poland remained divisive. Stalin made it clear he meant to keep what the Red Army conquered and that for the Soviets Poland was a life-or-death issue. Churchill privately admitted that he could do little on the country's behalf.

The time had also come to deal with postwar Germany. Churchill had changed his mind and now hoped to use a democratic Germany to counterbalance Soviet power. He came out against the earlier agreements to divide the country and strip it of its industry. Nor did he support making the Germans pay war reparations, particularly the multibillion figure Stalin quoted. In the end, nothing was decided.

Despite the differences, Yalta was the peak of the alliance. The Allies could at last see the fruits of their efforts to defeat Germany, and hope remained that Roosevelt's proposed United Nations could build a lasting peace. Stalin had reached a personal peak. Less than thirty years after the humiliating Treaty of Brest-Litovsk in 1917, the Soviet Union was now a global power.

Hitler committed suicide on April 30, 1945, as Germany collapsed. At war's end, the Allies, joined by France, occupied four separate zones of the country, with the Soviets taking Berlin and the east. As agreed, the USSR declared war on Japan. But the Pacific war ended in August, after the American atomic bombings of Hiroshima and Nagasaki.

A victory parade was held on June 24 in Red Square. Stalin reviewed it from his usual spot atop the Lenin Mausoleum. As a hard rain fell, row upon row of troops and tanks passed to the crowd's cheers and beating drums. Two hundred Red Army veterans halted at the Mausoleum. There they threw captured German banners at Stalin's feet. That day, at least, Stalin received his people's honest and heartfelt gratitude. By the end of the celebrations, he had taken the new titles "Hero of the Soviet Union" and "Generalissimo."

Ten
SPHERES OF INFLUENCE

At least 26 million Soviet citizens died in World War II, far more than any in other nation. Those that survived had little to eat except cabbage and potatoes, and hundreds of thousands lived in ruins or holes in the ground. Women and children worked in the factories; old women plowed the fields. To reconstruct the devastated country in a humane way required patience and money. Stalin had neither. Instead, he used what he had in the past to rapidly rebuild—terror.

First he had to reestablish basic control. Outside the cities the countryside had returned to its pre-Soviet way of life. Peasant customs, culture, and a revival of market-style local economies had returned as Soviet institutions collapsed in war. Meanwhile, pro-independence guerillas in areas recently absorbed by the USSR continued to fight the Red Army. Resistance was fiercest in Ukraine and in the Baltic nations of Estonia, Latvia, and Lithuania.

Perhaps the greatest potential for unrest, however, came from ordinary Soviet citizens. Having sacrificed and endured so much, they hoped Stalin would allow government reforms and that life might get a little easier. Instead, the government began to reassert control.

One of the worst of Stalin's cruelties was his treatment of returning Soviet prisoners of war (POWs). "That spring of 1945 was, in our prisons, predominately the spring of the Russian prisoner of war," wrote Alexander Solzhenitsyn. The POWs, having survived horrifying years in German camps, returned home to interrogation and torture, to long sentences in the gulags or the firing squad.

This inhuman treatment of the returning POWs had a perverse basis in history. Stalin knew that in the early 1800s Russian officers had returned from other wars influenced by European ideas. A few years later, a group of them had revolted against the czar in hopes of encouraging reforms. Stalin feared the same thing might happen again. Millions of Soviet citizens had caught a glimpse of life outside the USSR. They had seen the relative plenty produced in the capitalist countries. For this reason they had to be quarantined from the rest of Soviet society.

Stalin treated non-Russian ethnic groups with special brutality. The war had revived nationalism in the

Although this postwar, pro-veteran propaganda poster declares "Glory to the defenders of Moscow," many Soviet soldiers returned home to a hostile environment under Stalin. (Library of Congress)

provinces. Early in the war Stalin had even encouraged it. He knew Ukrainians, Azerbaijanis, Georgians, and all the rest would fight harder for their vague idea of a homeland than they would for the Soviet government. Members of several ethnic groups, however, had aided the Germans.

In 1944, with the war still raging, Stalin sent his trusted lieutenant Beria south, with trainloads of soldiers, militia, and NKVD officers, to the Caucasus Mountains to stamp out nationalistic uprisings. Beria began by packing off over 37,000 Balkars to Central Asia and Siberia via train and truck. Soon the government deported millions of Chechens, Ingush, Tatars, Bulgarians, Azerbaijanis, Armenians, as well as the area's Jewish and Muslim populations. Conditions were terrible. One estimate is that a third of the five million deportees died, either during transport or once they reached the remote, poorly prepared areas of exile. The Baltic countries endured similar treatment. After destroying the independence movements there, Stalin ordered in the secret police, and thousands of Estonians, Latvians, and Lithuanians—in particular politicians, intellectuals, and clergy—were killed or sent away.

Meanwhile, the postwar international situation quickly grew tense. Relationships with the wartime allies had begun to worsen almost from the moment the Germans surrendered. In July 1945, the Allies met for the last time at Potsdam, Germany. This time Stalin was the elder statesman. Roosevelt had died in April and was replaced by Harry S Truman. In the middle of the summit, Churchill returned home for elections and was thrown out of office. His replacement, Clement Atlee, represented Britain in the second half of the talks.

Truman had maneuvered the conference dates to coincide with America's first atomic bomb test. Three days after he learned the results, he shared the news of the weapon with Stalin. The Soviet leader appeared unmoved. Many interpreted that to mean Stalin knew nothing about atomic weapons. In fact, he had already

Longtime Stalin crony Lavrenti Beria, featured on the cover of Time *in 1953, eventually would be executed by Stalin's successors.* (Courtesy of Getty Images.)

heard about the successful test through his spy network. Unknown to the Allies, the Soviet Union had begun its own atomic-bomb program three years earlier.

The top-secret project—code-named Task Number

One—was under the control of Beria, who brought a ruthless efficiency to the atomic bomb project. He had control over the vast gulag system, and slave labor was used in the project. And as head of the NKVD, he had dealt with foreign espionage. That was essential, because the success of the Soviet program depended in large part on data stolen from other countries, particularly the U.S.

The Soviets considered the United States' atomic bombings of Hiroshima and Nagasaki a setback. Stalin had expected to emerge from the war as the dominant power in the world. Instead, the wealthiest capitalist nation had sole possession of the world's deadliest weapon. One of the Soviet scientists described the mood: "The Soviet government interpreted [Hiroshima] as atomic blackmail against the USSR, as a threat to unleash a new, even more terrible and devastating war." Stalin recognized he had to overcome the American nuclear advantage if the Soviet Union was to take its place as a world power.

Stalin considered a Soviet bomb essential to his country's survival. But the program contributed to the already-lean lives of Soviet citizens. It took massive amounts of the government's limited money to maintain the necessary support system of factories, mining concerns, power stations, advanced industrial processes, laboratories, and top-secret "atomic cities." Because of the bomb, the government neglected priorities such as housing, agriculture, higher wages, and consumer goods.

In the meantime, foreign-policy issues drove the Allies further apart. Germany's future topped the list of tension spots. Stalin was sure Germany would rebound sooner rather than later. Despite his worries, Stalin, for a time, seemed willing to let the country reunite—provided he found its new government friendly.

Stalin held back from turning Germany's eastern zone into a Soviet satellite. He agreed to allow the democracies to aid the rebuilding of German industry in their zones—as long as some of the goods went to the Soviet Union as war reparations. To the Americans, this looked like an attempt to siphon off U.S. aid, and Truman refused. The Soviets had to be satisfied with dismantling eastern Germany's factories and shipping them back to the USSR. A number of German specialists, including scientists skilled in nuclear physics, went along.

The fate of Eastern Europe was, from Stalin's point of view, less open to debate. The Red Army had liberated most of the countries there. Therefore, the Soviet Union had the final say on their postwar direction. Having thought so often of spreading revolution and creating Socialist allies, the Soviets were not going to give up this opportunity. The situation looked promising. Even in countries where the Red Army played a minimal role (or none at all), Communist parties enjoyed wide support. In Yugoslavia and Greece, Communist guerillas had led the fight against German occupation. Czechoslovakia, having been betrayed to Nazi Germany in 1938 by Britain and France, listened to Soviet proposals. Stalin envisioned a Red empire that stretched from the Pacific to Berlin, from Estonia to the borders of Turkey and Iran.

Stalin believed he had every right to expand. The evidence of two world wars proved that the USSR needed friendly countries on its borders to protect itself. To his mind the Allies were no different. "The United Kingdom had India and the Indian Ocean in her sphere of interest," he said. "The United States [had] China and Japan; the USSR had nothing." That this new empire depended on military force rather than Marxist class conflict did not matter. New theories could be invented.

In February 1947, Britain informed the U.S. it planned to give up support for anti-Communist movements in Greece and Turkey. Truman convinced the U.S. Congress to step into Britain's place. As part of his campaign, he explained his new policy to contain the spread of communism in what became known as the Truman Doctrine. Soon after, the Americans announced the Marshall Plan, a massive aid program for the reconstruction of Europe. When much of Eastern Europe reacted favorably to the promised aid, Stalin put his foot down. Nations from Finland to Albania were instructed to reject the Marshall Plan. As a response to the Marshall Plan and the Truman Doctrine, Stalin began to place pro-Soviet governments in the capitals of Eastern Europe.

Most of the region's Communist parties did not give Stalin much to work with. Before the war, the local fascist and nationalist regimes had hunted them down, and during the German occupation, Nazi security

DEPARTMENT OF STATE
WASHINGTON

May 23, 1947

S̶E̶C̶R̶E̶T̶

MEMORANDUM FOR THE PRESIDENT

Subject: Proposed Agreement on Aid
to Greece

I am attaching for your consideration a proposed basic agreement between the United States and Greece setting forth the general terms and conditions which shall govern the furnishing of assistance to Greece by the United States.

I am also attaching a draft note which we would propose that the Greek Government send to this Government, in advance of the conclusion of the basic agreement, outlining the plans of the Greek Government which will lay a basis for American assistance in recovery and reconstruction in Greece. This note is incorporated by reference in an appropriate manner in the proposed basic agreement. Both the agreement and the note will be registered with the United Nations.

Under this proposed procedure, the initiative and responsibility for domestic reconstruction measures in Greece lie with the Greek Government where they belong, while at the same time the United States Government exercises full control over the expenditure of United States funds and over Greek governmental programs intimately affecting the success of the American assistance program.

If you approve the draft agreement and note, Secretary Marshall intends to send them immediately to Athens for discussion and negotiation with the Greek Government.

DEAN ACHESON

Enclosures:

Draft agreement.
Draft note.

This memo from U.S. secretary of state Dean Acheson to President Truman, regarding American aid to Greece, is one page of hundreds regarding the negotiations of the terms of the Truman Doctrine. (National Archives)

services had done the same, only more efficiently. Little remained of the prewar parties and new Communist parties had to be built from scratch. Furthermore, they had to gain at least a little popularity with ordinary citizens. In most countries, the prospect of living under Communist control was unpopular.

To ensure success, local Communist parties, helped by the Soviets, rigged the elections. Once agreeable governments were in place, the countries were put through Stalinist-style revolutions from above—the grim march of collectivization and industrialization followed by purges and show trials for Communist Party members, and terror and repression for everyone else.

Yugoslavia, however, resisted Stalin's plans for a monolithic Soviet bloc. The Yugoslavs had defeated the Germans without significant help from the Red Army. The proud and independent Yugoslav Communists, led by Josip Tito, refused to accept Soviet domination. Stalin was furious at their attitude. "I shall shake my little finger," he said, "and there will be no Tito."

He shook quite a bit more than one finger. First he tried propaganda. Titoism soon became a slur on a par with Trotskyism. When words failed, Stalin prohibited trade with the country and massed Red Army troops on its border. Yet Tito refused to knuckle under. So many Soviet assassins came after him that he felt it necessary to write the Soviet leader:

> Stalin. Stop sending assassins to murder me. We have already caught five, one with a bomb, another with a rifle. . . . If this doesn't stop, I will send one man to Moscow and there will be no need to send another.

Defiant of Stalin, Josip Tito ruled Yugoslavia independently of the Soviet bloc, from the end of World War II until his death in 1980. (Library of Congress)

Not only did the Yugoslav Communists survive, they inspired similar defiance across Eastern Europe. Tito rubbed more salt in the wound by accepting aid from the West.

After 1947, a series of events accelerated tensions between the USSR and the West. Stalin wanted to control all of Berlin, which was divided into sectors, east and west. His attempt to starve West Berlin into submission failed when the U.S. and Britain airlifted supplies into the city.

Then, on August 29, 1949, the Soviets successfully tested an atomic bomb. "It would have been a great misfortune if it hadn't worked," the thrilled Beria said in an understatement. The test came around the same time as the Communist victory in China's long civil war. It seemed Marxist revolution was on the march to world-wide victory.

The successful bomb test was good news, but Stalin was not lulled into a false euphoria. The tense international situation escalated into a mania for security that led inevitably to more terror. Stalin's associates who had survived the 1930s saw parallels with that earlier time. Stalin began by going after his marshals and generals. As the victors over Germany, the Red Army's military leaders were popular war heroes. To Stalin, however, they represented a pool of potential replacements.

General Zhukov, a hero of the Soviet Union and savior of Moscow, was interrogated and reassigned to second-rate commands far from Moscow. His name, and that of numerous other marshals and generals, disappeared from the media and government proclamations. Zhukov and others who had their careers derailed were lucky; some of their comrades-at-arms were imprisoned or shot.

In another parallel to the 1930s, Stalin lashed out at the intelligentsia and artists. For this he used Andrei Zhdanov, the wartime leader of Leningrad and, of late, Stalin's enforcer in postwar Finland. Many considered him Stalin's likely successor, until Zhdanov died suddenly in 1948 under suspicious circumstances. Stalin might have had him killed and, just as before, he would use the death as an excuse to arrest others. Quietly, the gulags began to fill up. By 1950, over 2.5 million prisoners were inside, a record number at that time.

Stalin was aging rapidly. His thoughts wandered, his breath was sometimes short, and the chest pains stabbed. Arthritis and hardening of the arteries tormented him, and heavy smoking aggravated his heart problems. He sometimes had trouble speaking. His workaholic habits had always limited his exercise, but now even his walks around the Kremlin neighborhood were a thing of the past because of rheumatism.

As he entered the last years of his life, the Soviet dictator was more isolated than ever. Much of his socializing was with his bodyguards or housekeeper, or with nervous lieutenants trying to stay awake during late-night movies followed by massive buffet dinners and drinking binges. A lot of critical decisions were made at these parties, between practical jokes and boozing and the insults that betrayed the rivalries within Stalin's entourage.

He was restless and his mood swings became more extreme, the anger and suspicions more intense and less predictable. Stalin's emotional state certainly contributed to the purges of the late 1940s and early 1950s, but was not the only reason. As in the original purges, the regime's failures at home and internationally had to be blamed on enemies and conspiracies.

The United States, entering one of the most prosperous periods in its history, was leaving the Soviet economy behind. From the Soviet viewpoint this was infuriating and dangerous. They could justifiably put part of the blame on the destructive war. But the command economy, and Stalin's relentless pressure to rebuild at all cost, created a great deal of waste and unnecessary suffering. Gulag labor was expensive and did not produce as much as free workers. Prisoners were poorly treated, badly fed, and without adequate medical care.

Command economies are slow to adapt to change, unlike more flexible capitalist systems. Soviet bureaucracy was stifling; decisions had to be passed up through many levels of bureaucrats and, once a decision was made, had to take the same long journey back down. Corruption was rampant. Administrators stole and falsified critical statistics to hide mistakes. Officials promoted family and friends regardless of competence. Yet Stalin refused to believe the system was flawed, instead blaming saboteurs and foreign spies for problems.

Stalin's own immense power also got in the way. As powerful as he was, he could not keep track of everything and had to make decisions based on falsely optimistic reports. No one wanted to bring Stalin bad news. "[He] knew the country and agriculture only from films," Nikita Khrushchev, a future Soviet leader, said. "And these films had dressed up and beautified the existing situation." Stalin delegated the bulk of the work to his lieutenants and then interfered with their decisions whenever he pleased.

As the West prospered, Stalin tightened the curtain around the USSR and its satellite states in Eastern Europe. Nothing was allowed to contradict the propaganda that praised the country's accomplishments and the exalted wisdom of its leader.

The campaign of Soviet and Russian glorification became almost surreal. The Soviet Union and czarist

Russia became the source from which all human progress came. Russians, not the Wright Brothers, invented the airplane, as well as the radio and television. The fact that other nations claimed these inventions only proved how much they envied the superior Russian culture. Sometimes this propaganda reached comical proportions. When President Truman sent him Coca-Cola as a gift, Stalin angrily demanded that Soviet scientists come up with a superior beverage made from pears.

This celebration of Russian nationalism made some of the darker aspects of Russian culture acceptable again. For centuries, Jews had provided a scapegoat and a distraction from the czars' own failures. The Soviet government began to encourage anti-Semitism for the same reasons. The press pushed the idea that Jews were people without a country because their loyalty could not be trusted. When Israel declared independence in 1948 and allied with the U.S., Soviet propaganda emphasized that Jews were loyal only to Israel.

As before, Stalin slowly maneuvered political associates into vulnerable positions. He first turned against the younger, more independent members of the party elite. His closest lieutenants began to sense the danger to themselves, and none more than Molotov, his long-time right-hand man. In 1948, Stalin ordered the arrest of Polina Molotova, Molotov's Jewish wife. Interrogators tried to connect her to Jewish nationalists, a new group of enemies of the people. But her Judaism was cultural, not religious—like all good Communists she was an atheist. Molotov lost his position as head of Foreign Affairs and his standing invitation to dinner at Stalin's house. Having fallen out of favor, he stood to lose much more.

Stalin's men knew that if the dictator could turn on Molotov, he could turn on anyone. "In those days anything could have happened to any of us," Khrushchev said. "Bulganin [another Soviet leader] once described very well the experience. . . . We were leaving Stalin's after dinner one night and he said, 'You come to Stalin's table as a friend, but you never know if you'll go home by yourself or if you'll be given a ride—to prison!'"

The party called a new congress, the first in years, for 1952. Stalin felt too ill to give the main report, but near the end he managed a six-minute speech that proposed turning the Politburo into a larger leadership group called the Presidium. To the surprise of many, he had already drawn up the list of members. No one dared argue, even when they learned he had named a number of younger men in addition to his old associates. His older lieutenants realized he meant to eliminate the current leadership. The younger men on the Presidium list would be their replacements.

Stalin continued to manufacture conspiracies. On November 4, 1952, he ordered the arrest and torture of Professor Vladimir Vinogradov, the family doctor at the Kremlin. This so-called Doctor's Plot was Stalin's attempt to weave anti-Semitism, the elimination of his lieutenants, foreign spies, Titoism, and the usual scapegoats into a vast new conspiracy that had to be destroyed.

On January 13, 1953, *Pravda* announced that nine doctors, six of them Jewish, had admitted to the murder of Zhdanov and to plotting the murders of other party leaders. They also confessed to being spies for the United States and Great Britain. The revelation exploded into a new mania of anti-Semitism and xenophobia.

But this time, Stalin's monomania was cut short. On the night of February 28, he met with his lieutenants at his house for a late dinner. The guests left around four in the morning, and Stalin fell asleep on a divan in the dining room. Then, sometime on March 1, he had a stroke. His guards, afraid to disturb him, did not check on him until 10:00 PM. One of them found the Soviet leader on the floor unable to speak. After making him comfortable on a sofa, they called the secret police chief. When Stalin's lieutenants arrived in the predawn hours, they insisted he was merely sleeping and left. The guards, who would be blamed if he died, demanded doctors be called in. The doctors pronounced him a hopeless cause.

By March 4, he was fading. His children and lieutenants gathered around him the next day. "The death agony was terrible," his daughter Svetlana wrote.

> At what seemed like the very last moment, he suddenly opened his eyes and cast a glance over everyone in the room. It was a terrible glance, either

insane or perhaps angry and full of [the] fear of death. . . . He suddenly lifted his left hand as though he were pointing to something up above and bringing down a curse on us all.

Then the Man of Steel took a last breath and died.

His henchmen began destroying any documents that implicated them in his crimes. During the search they discovered three unusual pieces of paper in his desk: Lenin's demand for an apology to his wife; Tito's assassination threat; and Bukharin's dying plea, "Why do you need my life, Stalin?"

Stalin's embalmed body on display. (Library of Congress)

After it was embalmed, Stalin's body was displayed beside Lenin's at the mausoleum. Thousands came from every corner of the nation to mourn him. At one point a stampede in Red Square killed dozens of people.

Even in the oppressive culture of the Soviet Union, it did not take long before Stalin's crimes were exposed and his legend deflated. Only three years after his death, at the Twentieth Party Congress of the Soviet Communist Party in 1956, Nikita Khrushchev shocked his audience and the world by denouncing Stalin as a tyrant and monster who had sent thousands of innocent people to their deaths. Khrushchev, who had his own political need to separate himself from his participation in Stalin's activities, claimed he needed to expose the crimes before they became known throughout the world.

Khrushchev promised that under his leadership, the Soviet Union was entering a more humane era. He ordered Stalin's body removed from its place of honor in Lenin's Mausoleum.

Under Khrushchev, there was a temporary easing of restrictions within the Soviet Union, but that soon came to an end. He was pushed out of power in 1964, and the Soviet Union entered into a long period during which the government stifled dissent while focusing on building up the industrial base and challenging the democratic West in the Cold War. By the last decade of the twentieth century, the Soviet Union had collapsed and the Marxist experiment, for which millions of Soviet citizens had lost their lives, was over.

GLOSSARY

Bolsheviks
A faction of the Russian Social Democratic Workers Party
united behind V. I. Lenin and his interpretation of Marxist ideas.

Central Committee
In the USSR, the body in charge of policy and electing the
Politburo. During the Stalin era, however, the Politburo guided
much of the policy agenda.

Cheka
The early version of the Soviet secret police; later the GPU,
NKVD, MVD, MGB, and KGB.

Collectivization
The process of reorganizing Soviet agriculture from individu-
ally owned plots of land into collective farms (kohlkozes).

Communist Party (of the Soviet Union)
In the Soviet Union, the ruling political party led first by Lenin
that grew out of the Bolshevik faction of the Russian Social
Democratic Workers Party.

Gulag

Initially, GULAG was an acronym for the Main Camp Administration, the prison camp system operated by the Soviet secret police. The term gulag soon became a synonym for the camps themselves.

Kohlkoze

A collective farm. In theory, a kohlkoze was owned by all of its members collectively. Each kohlkoze had to pay part of what it produced to the Soviet government.

Kulak

The class of better-off peasants in rural Russia. During the Stalin era, however, the term was often applied to any peasant opposed to collectivization.

Mensheviks

A faction of the Russian Social Democratic Workers Party that took more traditional and moderate views of Marxist ideas than those proposed by Lenin and the Bolsheviks.

New Economic Policy (NEP)

Lenin's policy, begun in the early 1920s, of allowing a limited market economy, including private ownership of small- and medium-sized industry. The Soviet government kept ownership of large industry and most foreign trade, as well as overall control of the economy.

NKVD

The Soviet secret police organization from the early 1930s to the mid-1940s.

Okhrana
The Russian government's secret police organization under the czar.

Politburo
Also known as the Political Bureau, the Politburo was the elite body at the top of the Soviet government, elected by the Central Committee.

Pravda (Truth)
The major Bolshevik newspaper and later the major newspaper of the Soviet Union.

Provisional Government
The interim government formed by the Duma after the fall of the czar. The Bolsheviks overthrew the government in the October Revolution of 1917.

Russian Social Democratic Workers Party (RSDWP)
Russia's major Marxist political party, divided between two major factions, the Bolsheviks and Mensheviks, and with a small number of freelancers taking neither side.

Social Democrats (SDs)
The shorthand version of the Russian Social Democratic Workers Party (RSDWP).

Socialism in One Country
Stalin's theory that the Soviet Union could build a Socialist society without other Marxist nations as allies.

Soviets
Councils formed by industrial workers, particularly in St. Petersburg/Petrograd and Moscow, and usually organized and led by members of revolutionary political parties. Later, the term Soviet came to refer to a citizen of the Soviet Union.

Tiflis
The capital of Georgia, where Stalin attended seminary; the Georgian name is Tbilisi.

USSR
The Union of Soviet Socialist Republics, also known as the Soviet Union.

Whites
The catchall term for the armies and individuals opposed to Bolshevik rule during the Russian Civil War.

TIMELINE

1878	Joseph Vissarionovich Djugashvili is born on December 6.
1888	Enters Gori's religious elementary school.
1894	Attends the Tiflis Seminary on a full scholarship; joins a secret Socialist group at the school.
1899	Expelled from the seminary; takes a clerk's job at the Tiflis observatory.
1902	Arrested for the first time and sentenced to three years' exile in Siberia.
1910	Returned to Siberia after another escape; the next year his sentence ends, and he settles in Vologda.
1912	Made a member of the Bolshevik Central Committee.
1913	Goes to Vienna to write his first major work of theory; upon returning to Russia, he is arrested and sentenced to four years in the Arctic.
1917	Returns to Petrograd shortly after the czar abdicates.
1918	The Russian civil war begins; Stalin uses brutal methods to stabilize the situation in Tsaritsyn.
1919	White armies threaten Petrograd and Moscow; Stalin marries Nadya Alliluyeva.
1922	Stalin becomes general secretary.

1923	Lenin suffers a catastrophic stroke; Zinoviev and Kamenev ally with Stalin against Trotsky.
1924	Lenin dies.
1926-1927	Over two years, Stalin decisively defeats his opposition to total power in Russia: Trotsky, Zinoviev, and Kamenev.
1929	"Dekulakization" launches Stalin's collectivization of agriculture.
1932	Nadya Alliluyeva, Stalin's wife, commits suicide.
1937	Stalin appoints Nikolai Yezhov head of the NKVD, launching the most intense period of the Great Terror.
1939	The Soviet Union negotiates a nonaggression pact with Nazi Germany; World War II begins.
1941	Stalin goes into seclusion following the German invasion of the USSR; Soviet troops later defeat the Germans outside Moscow.
1943	Stalin meets Roosevelt and Churchill at Teheran; Stalin's son Yakov dies in a POW camp.
1945	Allied leaders meet again at Yalta and Potsdam; World War II ends.
1949	The USSR explodes an atomic bomb.
1952	Stalin plans the Doctor's Plot as the prelude to a new terror.
1953	Suffers a stroke March 1; dies on March 5.

Sources

CHAPTER ONE: Student Revolutionary

p. 17, "undeserved dreadful . . ." Robert C. Tucker, *Stalin As Revolutionary: A Study in History and Personality, 1879-1929* (New York: W. W. Norton, 1973), 73.

p. 17, "The early death . . ." Ibid., 73.

p. 18, "I don't know what . . ." Isaac Deutscher, *Stalin: A Political Biography,* 2nd ed. (New York: Oxford University Press, 1967), 3.

p. 18, "Soso's favorite game . . ." Edvard Radzinsky, *Stalin,* trans. H. T. Willetts (New York: Doubleday, 1996), 28.

p. 20, "He was always . . ." Tucker, *Stalin As Revolutionary,* 76-77.

p. 21-22, "In protesting against . . ." Bertram D. Wolfe, *Three Who Made a Revolution* (Boston: Beacon, 1955), 411.

p. 22, "touchy character," Tucker, *Stalin As Revolutionary*, 84.

p. 22, "We would sometimes . . ." Deutscher, *Stalin,* 17.

p. 23, "Koba had become . . ." Alan Bullock, *Hitler and Stalin: Parallel Lives* (New York: Vintage, 1993), 7.

p. 27, "We had to keep . . ." Edward Ellis Smith, *The Young Stalin* (New York: Farrar, Straus and Giroux, 1967), 68-69.

p. 27, "This lack of compromise . . ." Svetlana Alliluyeva, *One More Year,* trans. Paul Chavchavadze (New York: HarperCollins, 1969), 377.

CHAPTER TWO: What Is To Be Done?

p. 29, "I visited Koba . . ." Radzinsky, *Stalin,* 47.

p. 32, "There is no other . . ." Wolfe, *Three Who Made a Revolution,* 229.

p. 33-34, "He worshipped Lenin..." Radzinsky, *Stalin,* 47.

p. 41, "I had hoped to see . . ." Deutscher, *Stalin,* 78.

p. 43, "Koba firmly pressed . . ." Tucker, *Stalin As Revolutionary,* 108.

CHAPTER THREE: From Exile to Revolution

p. 47, "With me is the Georgian . . ." Tucker, *Stalin As Revolutionary,* 158.

p. 47, "We know each other . . ." Roy Medvedev, *Let History Judge: The Origins and Consequences of Stalinism,* rev. ed., trans. and ed. George Shriver (New York: Columbia University Press, 1989), 36.

p. 50-51, "social revolution . . . even be forseen," Richard Pipes, *The Russian Revolution* (New York: Knopf, 1990), 211.

p. 54, "War is not an accident . . ." William Henry Chamberlin, *The Russian Revolution,* vol. 1, *1917-1918* (Princeton, NJ: Princeton University Press, 1987), 128.

p. 55-56, "[T]he strain is so great . . ." Ibid., 67.

p. 56, "Hurry up and finish . . ." W. Bruce Lincoln, *Passage Through Armageddon: The Russians in War and Revolution, 1914-1918* (New York: Simon and Schuster, 1986), 316.

p. 56, "What revolution? . . ." Pipes, *The Russian Revolution,* 276.

p. 59, "He was still . . ." Radzinsky, *Stalin,* 89.

p. 61, "What's this you're . . ." Edmund Wilson, *To The Finland Station* (Garden City, NY: Doubleday, 1953), 466.

p. 61, "Lenin's general scheme . . ." Lincoln, *Passage Through Armageddon,* 365.

p. 63, "Now it is possible . . ." Chamberlain, *The Russian Revolution,* vol. 1, 184.

p. 64, "disgraceful," "criminal," "betrayal of . . ." Lincoln, *Passage Through Armageddon,* 429.

p. 68, "I was seated above . . ." V. M. Molotov with Felix Chuev, *Molotov Remembers,* ed. Albert Resis (Chicago: Ivan R. Dee, 1993), 96-97.

p. 70, "You are pitiful . . ." Leon Trotsky, *The History of the Russian Revolution,* vol. 3, *The Triumph of the Soviets* Trans. by Max Eastman (New York: Simon and Schuster, 1932), 311.

p. 71, "[Stalin] gave the . . ." Medvedev, *Let History Judge,* 44.

CHAPTER FOUR: Civil War

p. 74, "Comrade Trotsky's position . . ." Robert Service, *Stalin: A Biography* (Cambridge, MA: Harvard University Press, 2004), 159-160.

p. 74, "If you don't sign . . ." Lincoln, *Passage Through Armageddon,* 502.

p. 76, "Petrograd is in an . . ." Chamberlin, *The Russian Revolution,* vol. 1, 416.

p. 76, "[You say] the land . . ." W. Bruce Lincoln, *Red Victory* (New York: Simon and Schuster, 1989), 467.

p. 79, "For the good . . ." Tucker, *Stalin As Revolutionary,* 192-93.

p. 79, "I categorically insist . . ." Medvedev, *Let History Judge,* 58.

p. 85, "The greatest delight . . ." Tucker, *Stalin As Revolutionary,* 211.

p. 88, "Respected Comrade Stalin . . ." Bullock, *Hitler and Stalin,* 123.

p. 89, "Yet if you consider . . ." Service, *Stalin: A Biography,* 212.

CHAPTER FIVE: Stalin's Rise to Power

p. 92, "I knew only . . ." Leon Trotsky, *My Life: An Attempt at an Autobiography* (New York: Pathfinder, 1970), 509.

p. 94, "sufficient caution," Medvedev, *Let History Judge,* 80.

p. 94, "Stalin is too rude . . ." Ibid., 81.

p. 94-95, "Painful embarrassment . . ." Tucker, *Stalin As Revolutionary,* 289.

p. 96, "I came to Lenin . . ." Ibid., 336-37.

p. 100, "She was very beautiful . . ." Radzinsky, *Stalin,* 277.

p. 100, "It will be enough . . ." Deutscher, *Stalin,* 308.

p. 101, "The first [General] Secretary . . ." Isaac Deutscher, *The Prophet Unarmed: Trotsky, 1921-1929* (New York: Verso, 2003), 248.

p. 102, "That way . . ." Radzinsky, *Stalin,* 223.

CHAPTER SIX: The Second Revolution

p. 105, "To slacken the pace . . ." Service, *Stalin: A Biography,* 272-273.

p. 106-107, "It is not a matter . . ." Tucker, *Stalin As Revolutionary,* 414.

p. 107, "You and I . . ." Radzinsky, *Stalin,* 234.

p. 107, "[Stalin] is an . . ." Stephen F. Cohen, *Bukharin and the Bolshevik Revolution: A Political Biography, 1888-1938* (New York: Vintage, 1975), 286.

p. 109, "smash the *kulaks* . . ." Deutscher, *Stalin,* 320.

p. 112, "Collective farms cannot . . ." Ibid., 330.

p. 114, "A few steps further . . ." Miron Dilot, *Execution by Hunger: The Hidden Holocaust* (New York: W. W. Norton, 1985), 180.

p. 115, "It has cost . . ." Bullock, *Hitler and Stalin,* 270.

p. 115, "Ha! He couldn't . . ." Medvedev, *Let History Judge,* 299.

p. 116, "Hey you . . . dare 'hey' me!" Robert C. Tucker, *Stalin in Power: The Revolution from Above, 1928-1941* (New York: W. W. Norton, 1990) 216.

p. 116, "She left me . . ." Bullock, *Hitler and Stalin,* 368.

p. 116, "I had never . . ." Molotov, *Molotov Remembers,* 173.

p. 119, "best of the best . . ." Medvedev, *Let History Judge,* 321.

CHAPTER SEVEN: Enemies of the People

p. 121-122, "I never saw [Bukharin] . . ." Nadezhda Mandelstam, *Hope Against Hope,* tran. Max Hayward (New York: Atheneum, 1970), 22-23.

p. 123, "Why? . . . Ask them!" Simon Sebag Montefiore, *The Court of the Red Tsar* (New York: Knopf, 2004), 41.

p. 124, "If you do not . . ." Bullock, *Hitler and Stalin,* 962.

p. 126-127, "You say you don't . . ." Ibid., 359.

p. 128, "Soviet literature . . ." Tucker, *Stalin In Power,* 564.

p. 129, "Koba, why do you . . ." Robert Conquest: *The Great Terror: A Reassessment* (New York: Oxford University Press, 1990), 168.

p. 129, "Heavens, what a . . ." Ibid., 169.

p. 130, "I am not . . ." Cohen, *Bukharin and the Bolshevik Revolution,* 370.

p. 133, "For eventual arrest . . ." Conquest, *The Great Terror: A Reassessment,* 235.

p. 134, "Koba . . . why do . . ." Tucker, *Stalin In Power,* 500.

p. 135, "You're a good worker . . ." Montefiore, *The Court of the Red Tsar,* 503.

p. 136, "grave mistakes . . ." Conquest, *The Great Terror: A Reassessment,* 440.

CHAPTER EIGHT: The Road to Total War

p. 141, "They're not . . ." Montefiore, *The Court of the Red Tsar,* 307.

p. 142, "I have them! I have them!" Albert Speer, *Inside the Third Reich,* trans. Richard Winston and Clara Winston (New York: Macmillan, 1970), 161.

p. 142, "Of course . . ." Montefiore, *The Court of the Red Tsar,* 312.

p. 144, "The friendship . . ." Deutscher, *Stalin,* 445.

p. 145, "Couldn't they . . ." Montefiore, *The Court of the Red Tsar,* 334.

p. 147, "You're choking me," Deutscher, *Stalin,* 452.

p. 147-148, "entire thoughts and actions . . ." Gabriel Gorodetsky, *Grand Delusion: Stalin and the German Invasion of Russia* (New Haven, CT: Yale University Press, 1999), 244.

p. 148, "reported the situation . . ." Georgi K. Zhukov, *Memoirs of Marshal G. Zhukov* (New York: Delacorte, 1971), 235.

p. 148, "Hitler surely does . . ." Gorodetsky, *Grand Delusion,* 311.

p. 149, "Stalin said, 'We blew it . . ." Molotov, *Molotov Remembers,* 39.

p. 149, "cowards, panic-mongerers . . ." Deutscher, *Stalin,* 463.

p. 149, "The collective farmers . . ." Ibid.

p. 152, "Are you sure . . ." Zhukov, *Memoirs,* 339.

CHAPTER NINE: An Uneasy Alliance

p. 156, "All service personnel . . ." Radzinsky, *Stalin,* 475.

p. 158, "You are leaving . . . such a policy," Winston S. Churchill, *Memoirs of the Second World War,* abrid. ed. (Boston: Houghton Mifflin, 1959), 631.

p. 158, "My character . . . Motherland," Montefiore, *The Court of the Red Tsar,* 427.

p. 160, "I don't know..." Radzinsky, *Stalin,* 478.

p. 160, "Never once in . . ." Bullock, *Hitler and Stalin,* 815.

p. 163, "It was all settled . . ." Ibid., 866.

CHAPTER TEN: Spheres of Influence

p. 168, "That spring of 1945 . . ." Aleksandr Solzhenitsyn, *The Gulag Archipelago,* vol. 1., trans. Thomas P. Whitney (New York: Harper & Row, 1973), 237.

p. 172, "The Soviet government . . ." Vladislav Zubok and Constantine Pleshakov, *Inside the Kremlin's Cold War* (Cambridge, MA: Harvard University Press, 1996), 42.

p. 174, "The United Kingdom . . ." Robin Edmonds, *The Big Three: Churchill, Roosevelt, and Stalin in Peace and War* (New York: W. W. Norton, 1992), 413.

p. 176, "I shall shake . . ." Deutscher, *Stalin,* 594.

p. 176, "Stalin. Stop sending . . ." Roy Medvedev and Zhores Medvedev, *The Unknown Stalin: His Life, Death, and Legacy,* trans. Ellen Dahrendorf (New York: Overlook, 2003), 70.

p. 177, "It would have been . . ." Zubok and Pleshakov, *Inside the Kremlin's Cold War,* 151.

p. 180, "[He] knew the country . . ." Tucker, *Stalin In Power,* 567.

p. 182, "In those days . . ." Khrushchev, *Khrushchev Remembers,* 257-258.

p. 183-184, "The death agony . . . curse on us all," Bullock, *Hitler and Stalin,* 965.

BIBLIOGRAPHY

Alliluyeva, Svetlana. *One More Year*. Trans. Paul Chavchavadze. New York: HarperCollins, 1969.

Babel, Isaac. *1920 Diary*. Ed. by Carol J. Avins. Translated by H. J. Willetts. New Haven, CT: Yale University Press, 1990.

Beevor, Antony. *Stalingrad: The Fateful Siege, 1942-1943*. New York: Penguin, 1999.

Brent, Jonathan and Vladimir P. Naumov. *Stalin's Last Crime: The Plot Against the Jewish Doctors, 1948-1953*. New York, HarperCollins, 2003.

Brown, Clarence. *Mandelstam*. London: Cambridge University Press, 1973.

Bullock, Alan. *Hitler and Stalin: Parallel Lives*. New York: Vintage, 1993.

Chamberlin, William Henry. *The Russian Revolution*, 2 vols. Princeton, NJ: Princeton University Press, 1987.

Churchill, Winston S. *The Second World War*. Vol. VI: *Triumph and Tragedy*. Boston: Houghton Mifflin, 1953.

———. *Memoirs of the Second World War*. Abridged ed. Boston: Houghton Mifflin, 1959.

Cohen, Stephen F. *Bukharin and the Bolshevik Revolution: A Political Biography, 1888-1938*. New York: Vintage, 1975.

Conquest, Robert. *The Great Terror: A Reassessment*. New York: Oxford University Press, 1990.

———. *The Harvest of Sorrow: Soviet Collectivization and the Terror-Famine*. New York: Oxford University Press, 1986.

————. *Stalin and the Kirov Murder.* New York: Oxford University Press, 1989.

Deutscher, Isaac. *Stalin: A Political Biography.* 2nd ed. New York: Oxford University Press, 1967.

————. *The Prophet Armed: Trotsky, 1879-1921.* New York: Oxford University Press, 1954.

————. *The Prophet Unarmed: Trotsky, 1921-1929.* New York: Verso, 2003.

———— and David King. *The Great Purges.* Edited by Tamara Deutscher. New York: Basil Blackwell, 1984.

Dilot, Miron. *Execution By Hunger: The Hidden Holocaust.* New York: W. W. Norton, 1985.

Djilas, Miroslav. *Conversations With Stalin.* Translated by Michael B. Petrovich. New York: Harcourt, Brace & World, 1962.

Edmonds, Robin. *The Big Three: Churchill, Roosevelt, and Stalin in Peace and War.* New York: W. W. Norton, 1992.

Fischer, Louis. *The Life of Lenin.* New York: Harper & Row, 1964.

FitzLyon, Kyril, and Tatiana Browning. *Before the Revolution: A View of Russia Under the Czar.* Woodstock, NY: Overlook Press, 1978.

Getty, J. Arch and Oleg V. Naumov. *The Road to Terror: Stalin and the Self-Destruction of the Bolsheviks, 1932-1939.* New Haven, CT: Yale University Press, 1999.

Gorky, Maxim. *Untimely Thoughts: Essays on Revolution, Culture, and the Bolsheviks, 1917-1918.* Translated by Herman Ermolaev. New York: Paul S. Eriksson, 1968.

Gorodetsky, Gabriel. *Grand Delusion: Stalin and the German Invasion of Russia.* New Haven, CT: Yale University Press, 1999.

Grossman, Vasily. *Forever Flowing.* Translated by Thomas P. Whitney. Evanston, IL: Northwestern University Press, 1997.

Karny, Yo'av. *Highlanders: A Journey to the Caucasus in Quest of Memory.* New York: Farrar, Straus and Giroux, 2000.

Khrushchev, Nikita S. *Khrushchev Remembers.* Trans. by Strobe Talbott. New York: Little, Brown and Company, 1970.

King, David. *The Commissar Vanishes.* New York: Metropolitan Books, 1997.

Lang, David Marshall. *The Georgians.* New York: Frederick A. Praeger, 1966.

Larina, Anna. *This I Cannot Forget.* Trans. by Gary Kern. New York: W.W. Norton, 1993.

Lenin, V. I. *Selected Works.* Vol. 3. Moscow: Progress Publishers, 1971.

Lincoln, W. Bruce. *In War's Dark Shadow.* New York: Dial Press, 1983.

———. *Passage Through Armageddon: The Russians in War and Revolution, 1914-1918.* New York: Simon and Schuster, 1986.

———. *Red Victory: A History of the Russian Civil War.* New York: Simon and Schuster, 1989.

Mandelstam, Nadezhda. *Hope Against Hope.* Translated by Max Hayward. New York: Atheneum, 1970.

Mandelstam, Osip. *Fifty Poems.* Translated by Bernard Meares. New York: Persea Books, 1977.

Mayer, Arno J. *The Furies: Violence and Terror in the French and Russian Revolutions.* Princeton, NJ: Princeton University Press, 2000.

Medvedev, Roy. *Let History Judge: The Origins and Consequences of Stalinism, Revised Edition.* Translated and edited by George Shriver. New York: Columbia University Press, 1989.

——— and Zhores Medvedev. *The Unknown Stalin: His Life, Death, and Legacy.* Trans. by Ellen Dahrendorf. New York: Overlook, 2003.

Molotov, V. M., with Felix Chuev. *Molotov Remembers.* Edited by Albert Resis. Chicago: Ivan R. Dee, 1993.

Montefiore, Simon Sebag. *Stalin: The Court of the Red Tsar.* New York: Knopf, 2004.

Pasternak, Boris. *Poems, Second Edition.* Translated by Eugene M. Kayden. Yellow Springs, OH: Antioch Press, 1964.

Pipes, Richard. *The Russian Revolution.* New York: Knopf, 1990.

———. *Russia Under the Bolshevik Regime.* New York: Knopf, 1993.

Radzinsky, Edvard. *Stalin.* Trans. H. T. Willetts. New York: Doubleday, 1996.

Reed, John. *Ten Days that Shook the World.* London: Penguin, 1977.

Service, Robert. *Stalin: A Biography.* Cambridge, MA: Harvard University Press, 2004.

Smith, Edward Ellis. *The Young Stalin: The Early Years of an Elusive Revolutionary.* New York: Farrar, Straus and Giroux, 1967.

Solzhenitsyn, Aleksandr. *The Gulag Archipelago.* Vol. 1. Translated by Thomas P. Whitney. New York: Harper & Row, 1973.

Speer, Albert. *Inside the Third Reich.* Translated by Richard Winston and Clara Winston. New York: Macmillan, 1970.

Sukhanov, N. N. *The Russian Revolution 1917: A Personal Record.* Translated and edited by Joel Carmichael. New York: Oxford University Press, 1955.

Trotsky, Leon. *The History of the Russian Revolution.* Vol. 3, *The Triumph of the Soviets.* Trans. by Max Eastman. New York: Simon and Schuster, 1932.

———. *My Life: An Attempt at an Autobiography.* New York: Pathfinder Press, 1970.

————. *On Lenin: Notes Toward a Biography.* Translated by Tamara Deutscher. London: George G. Harrap & Co. Ltd., 1971.

Truman, Harry S *Memoirs.* Vol. 1, *Year of Decisions.* Garden City, NY: Doubleday, 1955.

Tucker, Robert C. *Stalin As Revolutionary: A Study in History and Personality, 1879-1929.* New York: W. W. Norton, 1974.

————. *Stalin In Power: The Revolution from Above, 1928-1941.* New York: W. W. Norton, 1990.

Ulam, Adam B. *Stalin: The Man and His Era.* Boston: Beacon Press, 1989.

Volkogonov, Dmitri. *Stalin: Triumph and Tragedy.* Translated by Harold Shukman. Rocklin, CA: Prima, 1996.

Walker, Martin. *The Cold War: A History.* New York: Henry Holt, 1993.

Wilson, Edmund. *To the Finland Station: A Study in the Writing and Acting of History.* Garden City, NY: Doubleday & Company, 1953.

Wolfe, Bertram D. *Three Who Made a Revolution.* Boston: Beacon, 1955.

Zhukov, Georgi K. *Memoirs of Marshal G. Zhukov.* New York: Delacorte, 1971.

Zubok, Vladislav, and Constantine Pleshakov. *Inside the Kremlin's Cold War.* Cambridge, MA: Harvard University Press, 1996.

WEB SITES

http://www.stalinsethniccleansing.com/nextnn.htm
This Web site complements a book (originally published in Polish) that collects firsthand accounts of Stalin's ethnic cleansing in that region. Excerpts and photographs are available online.

http://www.fordham.edu/halsall/mod/1946stalin.html
An online version of a March 1946 interview of Stalin conducted by the *New York Times.*

http://www.time.com/time/personoftheyear/archive/photohistory/stalin.html
Time magazine twice named Joseph Stalin Man of the Year (1939 and 1942). See why, here.

http://www.marxists.org/archive/trotsky/
Hosted by the Marxists Internet Archive, this page links to many online translations of Trotsky's writing.

http://www.hooverdigest.org/983/hahn.html
The Hoover Institution on War, Revolution and Peace, based at Stanford University, is a public-policy research center that has obtained and made available online a number of documents related to Stalin's Great Terror.

INDEX